CONVERSATIONS WITH

# ELIE WIESEL

# CONVERSATIONS WITH

# ELIE WIESEL

Elie Wiesel and Richard D. Heffner

*Edited by Thomas J. Vinciguerra*

SCHOCKEN BOOKS    NEW YORK

Copyright © 2001, 2003 by Elirion Associates, Inc.,
and Richard D. Heffner

All rights reserved under International and Pan-American
Copyright Conventions. Published in the United States by
Schocken Books, a division of Random House, Inc., New York,
and simultaneously in Canada by Random House of Canada
Limited, Toronto. Distributed by Pantheon Books, a division of
Random House, Inc., New York. Originally published
in slightly different form in hardcover in the United States
by Schocken Books, a division of Random House, Inc.,
New York, in 2001.

Schocken and colophon are registered
trademarks of Random House, Inc.

Library of Congress Cataloging-in-Publication Data

Wiesel, Elie, 1928–
Conversations with Elie Wiesel / Elie Wiesel and Richard D.
Heffner ; edited by Thomas J. Vinciguerra.
p.  cm.
ISBN 0-8052-1141-1
1. Wiesel, Elie, 1928—Interviews. 2. Authors, French—20th
century—Interviews. 3. Authors, American—20th century—
Interviews. I. Heffner, Richard D. II. Vinciguerra, Thomas J.
III. Title.

PQ2683.I32 Z4618 2001  [B]  2001020948

www.schocken.com

Book design by Cassandra J. Pappas

Printed in the United States of America
FIRST PAPERBACK EDITION
2  4  6  8  9  7  5  3  1

# Contents

# Contents

# Introduction

OF THE HUNDREDS of distinguished persons who have graced "The Open Mind" since I began to produce and moderate my weekly public television series in 1956, Elie Wiesel is unquestionably the one I most closely identify with the program's very purpose: to probe as deeply, as honestly, and as freely as concerned men and women can into both the clearly universal and the seemingly more personal issues that today must challenge all thoughtful individuals.

Surely his breadth of humanistic understanding, his profound wisdom, his always reassuring presence, together with the warmth of our personal relationship, have all combined to make him the program's quintessential guest. And the very degree to which Elie's beliefs are so deeply rooted in and reflect his Judaic tenets and traditions, while mine are quite so secular, has, I hope, added an important and provocative dimension to the quality of our exchanges as together we embrace John Milton's singular query: "Who ever knew Truth put to the worse, in a free and open encounter?"

Among the earliest of my on-the-air discussions with Elie was a segment entitled "Beyond the Holocaust." And indeed, although the Holocaust has necessarily informed all of his public appearances—how could it be otherwise?—it soon became clear to both of us that the thoughts Elie was sharing with me and our audience extended far beyond his continuing reflections on that uniquely horrific calamity. So with a view toward creating an offering of even more general public interest, we decided to undertake a series of special television and home-video "Dialogues" on more or less cosmic—though still profoundly personal—themes on which Elie very much wished to comment, and to which he invariably brought to bear the weight of a profoundly moral perspective clearly derived from his religious beliefs.*

Indeed, in explaining his point of view Elie had once pointedly commented to me on an "Open Mind" program that whatever we do must be measured in personal moral terms. That became the hallmark of our "Dialogues" to-gether, and each time I borrowed from my partner to intro-duce our discussions:

> Whatever paths nations follow or overarching choices mankind makes about issues that universally claim our attention, surely it is instead whatever individual men and women, you and we, decide and then do about these

*Elie Wiesel • Richard D. Heffner: "Dialogues: A Series of Conversations on the Crucial Issues of Our Times." A Production of Richard Heffner Associates, Inc. and Alvin H. Perlmutter, Inc., Distributed by SISU Home Entertainment Inc., Cherokee Station, P.O. Box 20405, New York, NY 10021

issues much closer to home and hearth that truly looms larger; so that whatever we do must be measured in personal moral terms.

The reader should know then that the eleven chapters herein were distilled from nearly two dozen half-hour "Open Mind"s and "Dialogues," as well as from discussions conducted specifically for this volume. Preparing this material for book form has, of course, presented many challenges. Transcripts can rarely be published intact. Digressions, false starts, and other such intrusions on narrative flow must be straightened out. Yet to do so by usual editorial standards might scar Elie's unique method of inquiry. While I ask questions, Elie so frequently answers them by asking still others.

Therefore, while as much of our original exchanges has been preserved as possible, at the same time liberties have been taken. Several of the themes Elie and I explored more than once have been integrated. Major portions and minor passages from different programs have been freely intermixed when they seemed to speak to each other. And on rare occasions conversations that led into territory from which there was no easy return have been excised.

Perhaps the biggest obstacle to overcome was the fleeting nature of the subject matter. As a glance at our chapter titles shows, these exchanges address some of the most vexing social and spiritual dilemmas of our times. However, the backdrop to these issues is a world that is ever changing. ("The events are too many, and they go very fast, too fast," Elie notes at one point.) So topics that no longer command our immediate attention have been dispensed with. And in the case of ongoing happenings like the strife in the former Yugoslavia and the Middle East, some of our more specific references have been modified to make them more general and enduring—all the while with the knowledge that events may yet overtake even our best intentions.

One of the happier results of this surgery has been the Interludes—those short Wiesel reflections found between the individual chapters. These were portions of our original programs that did not quite fit into the newly formed whole but were simply too compelling to toss aside. They offer memorable, often vivid insights into Elie's essential spirit, his incomparable understanding of the nature of human nature.

*Conversations with Elie Wiesel* takes us both back a good many years, through a generation of warm friendship and mutual respect, of affection, indeed of a brotherly love that I know we feel equally. Always—as I think our viewers have long realized, and as I hope our readers will, too—civility and a continuing search for the truth and for a sense of personal responsibility in framing our responses to challenges have characterized our work together.

In all of this cooperative endeavor, of course, particularly in the translation of the many years of my broadcast exchanges with Elie into the pointed *Conversations* that follow, I owe an unending debt of gratitude to the extraordinary editorial skills of my accomplished good friend and our indefatigable colleague Thomas J. Vinciguerra.

My thanks, too, to the Charles H. Revson Foundation and its president, Eli N. Evans, for generous support in the final preparation of this volume; to Daphne Doelger-

Dwyer, for hard work and unending patience that are always beyond the call of duty; and to my wife, Dr. Elaine Heffner, for trying so nobly to help me understand the traditions and beliefs she shares with our dear friend Elie Wiesel.

RICHARD D. HEFFNER
August 5, 2001

CONVERSATIONS WITH

# ELIE WIESEL

---

# ONE

# Am I My Brother's Keeper?

**Elie, this is a question that perhaps is not understood too well by a good many people in our time. What does it mean to you?**

It is a question that Cain asked of God, having killed Abel: "Am I my brother's keeper?" And the answer, of course, is, we are all our brothers' keepers. Why? Either we see in each other brothers, or we live in a world of strangers. I believe that there are no strangers in God's creation. There are no strangers in a world that becomes smaller and smaller. Today I know right away when something happens, whatever happens, anywhere in the world. So there is no excuse for us not to be involved in these problems. A century ago, by the time the news of a war reached another place, the war was over. Now people die and the pictures of their dying are offered to you and to me while we are having dinner. Since I know, how can I not transform that knowledge into responsibility?

So the key word is "responsibility." That means I must keep my brother.

**Yet it seems that despite the fact that we live in an age of rapid, immediate communications, we know so little about what is happening to our brothers.**

We are careless. Somehow life has been cheapened in our own eyes. The sanctity of life, the sacred dimension of every minute of human existence, is gone. The main problem is that there are so many situations that demand our attention. There are so many tragedies that need our involvement. Where do you begin? We know *too* much. No, let me correct myself. We are *informed* about too many things. Whether information is transformed into knowledge is a different story, a different question.

But we are in the world of communication. Nothing has caught the fantasy, the imagination, of the world these last years as communication has. So many radio stations, so many television stations, so many publications, so many talk shows. It's always more and more information that is being fed. And I'm glad that these things are happening, because I think people should be informed.

However, let us say that on a given day a tragedy has taken place. For a day we are all glued to the television. Three days later, we are still glued. A week later, another tragedy occurs and then the first tragedy is overshadowed by the next one. I remember when I saw the hungry children of Biafra for the first time. I didn't sleep. I tried everything I could to address the problem—to write articles and call up people and organize activities to send

4

food to those children. But if you had shown those pictures for a whole month, by the second month people would not have been moved by them. What happened to the information there? It is still stored, but yet we don't act upon it, because we are summoned by the current event.

**There seems to be almost an inevitability about what you are describing, because extending and perfecting the means of communications is certainly a major thrust of our times.**

I would like to be able to say to my students that there are so many things in the world that solicit your attention and your involvement that you can choose any one. I really don't mind where that particular event is taking place. But I would like my students to be fully involved in *some* event. Today, for instance, they will say, "I go to zone A, and then I go to zone B." But as long as zone A has not been covered fully, as long as it is a human problem, I don't think we can abandon it. All the areas must be covered. I would not want to live in a world today in which a person or a community, because of color, because of religion, because of ethnic origin, or because of social conditions, would feel totally neglected or abandoned. There must be someone who speaks to and for that group, every group.

**Is there any question but that we have seen the faces of those who suffer and yet we are not moved sufficiently?**

I plead your case: In 1945, all the newspapers and magazines in the United States showed the pictures of the concentration camps. And yet for another five years, displaced persons remained in those camps. How many were allowed to come to America? They were told,

"Those who want to go to Palestine, good. All the others, come and we shall give you what you really need most—human warmth"? Furthermore, look at what happened in South Africa. Apartheid was a blasphemy. We saw these white racists killing. I remember images that moved me to anger—images of funeral processions. Whites had killed blacks because they were black. And then the whites disrupted the funerals, killing more black people. That is the limit of endurance, the limit of any tolerance. We should have protested louder. And yet we didn't.

**We talk about a world that is, perhaps, too much with us, so much so that there is no time to focus. How do you help your students deal with that?**

I mentioned Cain and Abel. Why did Cain kill Abel? It is not because he was jealous. According to the text that we read and comment upon, it was because Cain spoke to Abel, his younger brother, and he told him of his pain, of his abandonment, of his solitude—that God didn't want to accept his offering. In the Bible it's said, "And Cain spoke to Abel." And we don't even know whether Abel listened. There was no dialogue. So the first act, really, among brothers, was a lack of communication.

So what I would teach my students is communication. I believe in dialogue. I believe if people talk, and they talk sincerely, with the same respect that one owes to a close friend or to God, something will come out of that, something good. I would call it presence. I would like my students to be present whenever people need a human presence. I urge very little upon my students, but that is one thing I do. To people I love, I wish I could say, "I will suffer in your place." But I cannot. Nobody can.

Nobody should. I can be present, though. And when you suffer, you need a presence.

**When you say "communicate," you mean to accept communication, don't you?**

To be able to give and to receive at the same time.

**Does it seem to you that we're not listening to the world around us, that we're so much involved in our individual pursuits?**

Absolutely. I think the noise around us has become deafening. People talk but nobody listens. People aren't afraid of that silence. Have you seen those youngsters and not-so-young people go around in the street with a Walkman on their ears? They don't want to hear anything. They want to hear only their own music. Which is the same music, by the way, that they heard yesterday. It's a kind of repetition which is deafening. People don't want to hear the world. The world is, I think, in need of being heard.

**Elie, I find that as I get older and older still, I so often find that I want to shut things out, because I can't focus on what needs to be focused on if I'm listening to everything. That seems to me to be where we began, in a sense.**

To me too, of course. So often I want to turn off everything and say, "Look, it's easier to talk about *Romeo and Juliet* than to talk about what's happening today anywhere in the world." Naturally. Because in that play, there is a text and there is a story. It's a story I can turn in any direction I want, really. You think that *Romeo and Juliet* is a story of love? It's a story of hate. So whatever subject I discuss, I can always turn it one way or another. It's familiar, graspable. I prefer to discuss Plato, naturally. But we must open our eyes, and—

I don't want to be a devil's advocate here. I understand the subjective need not to feel that I am my brother's keeper, the subjective need to shut out the pain—

Sure. You couldn't take it. There is a need to remember, and it may last only a day or a week at a time. We cannot remember all the time. That would be impossible; we would be numb. If I were to remember all the time, I wouldn't be able to function. A person who is sensitive, always responding, always listening, always ready to receive someone else's pain . . . how can one live? One must forget that we die; if not, we wouldn't live.

So what do we do? Can we both attend to our own needs and to the various needs of our family and friends and still extend the notion of "Am I my brother's keeper?" way beyond Abel to the far points of the world?

Perhaps we cannot, but we must try. Because we cannot, we must, even though Kant used to say, "We can, therefore we must." There is so much forgetfulness, so much indifference today, that we must fight it. We must fight for the sake of our own future. Is this the nature of human beings? Yes, it's part of our nature.

I know it all seems like too much—even in our own city, New York. There is so much hate and so much mistrust and distrust that you wonder what can reach these people who live together, who can live together, who after all must live together. Where do you begin? Now, I always feel very strongly about the person who needs me. I don't know who that person is, but if the person needs me, I somehow must think of that person more than about myself. Why? Because I see my own life in him or her. I remember there were times when I needed people, and they were not there. If there is a governing

precept in my life, it is that: If somebody needs me, I
must be there.

**When I ask the question that we began with—"Am I my
brother's keeper?"—I most often receive a blank stare.
Obviously that stare comes from people for whom the concept is, if not anathema, at least terribly foreign. More so
now, don't you think?**

More so, because it involves us more deeply, because it
goes further. If I say yes, then I have to do something
about it. Then it really goes further than that: What does
it mean? Who is my brother? It's a definition. Who is my
brother? Is any person in the street my brother? Is a person in Somalia my brother? Is a person in Armenia my
brother? Come on. If I say, "My brother," what do I
mean? Have I seen them? Have I met them? So of course
it could be a poetic expression, which means very little.
But if you say that there are people in the world who
need a brother, I will say, "Then I would like to be that
brother." I don't always succeed, of course. I cannot. I
am only an individual. I am alone, as you are alone.
What can we do? We can be the brother to one person
and then another person, to ten people, a hundred people in our whole life. Does it mean that we are brothers
to everybody in the world? No, we cannot be. So even if
we say that at least we can tell a story about a brother
who is looking for a brother and finds one, I think that's
quite enough.

**Yes, but aren't we experiencing a new kind of isolationism
today? "Please, I can't solve these problems. Don't burden
me with them. I'm not my brother's keeper!"**

Today brothers become strangers. How do you expect
strangers to become brothers? People who live in the

same country today are strangers to one another. Take what's happened in Eastern Europe when the reactionary, exclusionary forces rule. They are neighbors, close to one another, but they see in each other a threat, a source of suspicion, a conqueror, not a brother. I think it's an historical phenomenon, which is worrisome.

**Elie, what's the scriptural response to the question "Am I my brother's keeper?"**

It is actually written as a dialogue, a scenario. Cain kills Abel. And God says to him, "Hi, good morning, how are you?" "All right," says Cain. Then God says, "By the way, where is your brother?" "I don't know," is the answer. "What do you mean, you don't know?" asks God. The answer: "I don't know. Am I my brother's keeper?" And then God says, "Come on, you know. I hear the voice of your brother's blood coming from the bowels of the earth. And you want to cheat me." The whole thing is a little bit silly. Does it mean that God didn't know where Abel was? God is playing a game. It's simply a story which I like to interpret as meaning that it is possible, unfortunately, throughout history, for two brothers to be brothers and yet to become the victim and/or the assassin of the other. However, I go one step further and I try to teach my students that we learn another lesson: Whoever kills, kills his brother.

**Kills his brother or kills some part of himself?**

It's possible, as I interpret it, that Cain and Abel were only one person. Cain killed Abel in Cain.

**The Darwinian response to "Am I my brother's keeper?" is: "Of course not. If you pretend to be, you are interfering with natural selection." How do we build again upon the**

more ancient notion that indeed we are our brothers' keepers in many, many, ways?

But remember again, Cain was *not* his brother's keeper. He killed him.

**But the question asked by God—**

The question is good.

**I know that's your specialty—questions.**

I love questions, true. Because there is "quest" in "question." I love that. But today, I would like to put a face on words. When I see words, I see a face. When you speak about, let's say, "my brother's keeper," I see faces of people I knew or know, or people I've just seen this morning. Crossing the street, there is an old man with his hand outstretched. Now, am I his keeper?

**Are you?**

I must tell you that when I see that, I always feel strange. Because on the one hand, reason tells me that if I give him a dollar, he will go and buy alcohol. But then I say to myself, So what? Who am I to decide what he will do with the money that I give him? I cannot see an outstretched hand and not put something there. It's impossible. I know sometimes it's a weakness. I want to feel better, not to feel bad about it. But in fact I cannot.

**You talked about communications before. If we don't "listen" by providing, presumably our brother will rise up and strike us down.**

Or we would strike him down. Who are we? Children of Cain or children of Abel?

**What's your answer?**

You know, in my tradition, there is a marvelous way out. We are neither the children of Cain nor the children

of Abel. There was a third son that Adam and Eve had afterward called Seth. And we are children of Seth. Which means you can be both.

**Is that a cop-out?**

No, not really. I think we are always oscillating between the temptation for evil and an attraction to goodness. It's enough for me to close my eyes and remember what men are capable of doing to become terribly, profoundly, totally pessimistic, because they haven't changed. But then again, I open my eyes and close them again and say, "It would be absurd not to absorb some images and turn them into good consciousness." And it's up to us to choose. We are free to choose.

**Don't you think that in our country at this time we're less concerned with, have less compassion for, those who suffer?**

Absolutely. But it's really about what you are doing all your life. Can we really help more than the people around us? I go around the world, I travel, and whenever I hear about someone suffering, I try to go there and bear witness. That's my role, at least to bear witness. To say, "I've seen, I was there." Sometimes it inspires others to do what I am doing. More often than not, it doesn't.

**If the moral imperative that you pose is one that seemingly is rejected in our time, why do you maintain this posture: "We must be caring, rather than careless"?**

Because I don't have a position of power. Maybe that's the reason. You and I can afford to speak on moral issues. We don't have to make a decision on them. I am sure that if you had someone facing you here who had power, a senator or a member of the Cabinet, he or she would say, "We cannot do this or that." Why? "Because so much money would be needed. We don't have the money. Housing would be required. We don't have the housing." So I can afford, really, only to pose questions, and I know that.

**Yes, but I'm convinced that you raise questions because you know what the right moral answers are.**

That's true.

**And you believe that by raising those questions, we will come to those answers.**

I would like to think that. But even if I knew that I would not succeed, I would still raise those questions.

**Why?**

Otherwise, why am I here? I have the feeling, honestly, that my life is an offering. I could have died every minute between '44 and '45. So once I have received this gift, I must justify it. And the only way to justify life is by affirming the right to life of anyone who needs such affirmation.

**Aren't you affirming, too, a conviction that something will be done in response to your question?**

Here and there one person might listen and do something. Another person might listen and not do something. But I prefer to think that here and there there are small miracles. And there are: a good student, a good reader, a friend. I think we spoke about it years ago: Once upon a time, I was convinced I could change the whole world. Now I'm satisfied with small measures of grace. If we could open the door of one jail and free one innocent person . . . if I could save one child from starvation, believe me, to me it would be worth as much as, if not more than, all the work that I am doing and all the recognition that I may get for it.

You've spoken about those who put people in the death camps and brought about their deaths directly. You also speak about others who stood around indifferently. Do you feel that that is increasingly a theme in our own times?

Oh, more and more. I have the feeling that everything I do is a variation on the same theme. I'm simply trying to pull the alarm and say, Don't be indifferent. Simply because I feel that indifference now is equal to evil. Evil, we know more or less what it is. But indifference to disease, indifference to famine, indifference to dictators, somehow it's here and we accept it. And I have always felt that the opposite of culture is not ignorance; it is indifference. And the opposite of faith is not atheism; again, it's indifference. And the opposite of morality is not immorality; it's again indifference. And we don't realize how indifferent we are simply because we cannot *not* be a little bit indifferent. We cannot think all the time of all the people who die. If, while I sit with you, I could see the children who are dying now while we talk, we wouldn't be able to talk, you and I. We would have to take a plane, go there and do something. We wouldn't be able to continue to try to be logical and rational.

You've said that if we ignore suffering, we become accomplices, as so many did during the Holocaust. Where is it written that we are not moral accomplices?

But we are.

But what can you expect of us?

Learning. After all, I don't compare situations. I don't compare any period to the period of the Second World War. But we have learned something. I have the feeling that sometimes it takes a generation for an event to awaken our awareness. But if now, so many years after that event, we are still behaving as though it did not occur, then what is the purpose of our work as teachers, as writers, as men and women who are concerned with one another's lives?

**We have a tradition in this country of extending ourselves through our wealth, our material well-being. That tradition was set aside somewhat for some time. Do you think we will recapture it more fully?**

I hope so. I hope that there will be enough students and teachers and writers and poets and communicators to bring back certain values. If a father cannot feed his children, then his human rights are violated. We are such a wealthy society. I think of the United States and am overtaken by gratitude. This nation has gone to war twice in its history to fight for other people's freedoms. Then, after the wars, consider the economic help, the billions of dollars that we have given to those poor countries ravaged, destroyed by the enemy. And even now, what would the free world do without us? We have always been ready to help.

So why not? It would show that we still have compassion. Now, those are nice words, I know. But what else do we have? We have words, and sometimes we try to act upon them.

# INTERLUDE

---

IF I WERE TO INVOKE the past for the present, the present would be enriched. If you were to ask me what is the most important message, for instance, that I would like to communicate, it would be that we are all princes. And that comes from the Bible.

**The concept of the dignity of the individual?**

Sovereignty. We are all sovereign.

**How do you apply it to the issues that we face?**

Well, when I see a refugee coming to the border, to me that person is a king in exile. If I see a black person being persecuted, I feel it is a prince being oppressed. And that only makes my outrage deeper.

**What could the response be to the voice you raise?**

Oh, I know the response. They would say, "Well, he is dreaming." So why not? Physicians will tell you that without dreams, the body couldn't survive. Not only the mind but the body needs dreams. And if this is true of the body, how much more so of the spirit, or the soul?

# TWO

# The Intellectual in Public Life

**Have you ever, to your own satisfaction, defined what the role of the intellectual should be?**

I would, first of all, say that the role should be an improper one, so to speak. The intellectual should always be the one who questions, and therefore who questions himself or herself. An intellectual should not have power.

**Should not have power?**

It's dangerous. Because the intellectual likes to play with ideas. And in the process, he or she may see in people only ideas, which means abstractions. And therefore it's dangerous, because no human being is an abstraction. Every human being is more than an idea, more than the sum of all ideas. So the intellectual should be there, together with the person in power, and remind that person, "Wait, maybe what you are doing is not entirely correct. Maybe there is something else." Always to say, "Maybe there is an alternative."

**But that almost makes the intellectual the court jester.**

It depends on the text that the intellectual reads, in
effect, from his own mind. It also depends on the response of the person in power. If the person in power
sees in the intellectual the jester, then the intellectual
shouldn't be there, should leave, should seek another
ruler. But it need not be that way. It can be a meaningful
dialogue between a person of action and someone who
gives an articulation—an expression of and for that action.

**What about the intellectual in politics himself or herself?
We think of Woodrow Wilson. There have been comparatively few presidents of the United States who could be
broadly defined as intellectuals, but there have been many
leaders abroad who have been.**

The definition of "intellectual" is a complex one. Who
is an intellectual? Someone who has read a thousand
books? Someone who teaches? Someone who is being
taught? It is complicated. We would say the intellectual
is someone who sees reality in concepts, in the termi-
nology of possible ideas, one weighing against the other
or with the other, confronting one another. Wilson, yes,
but when he left Princeton, he already thought in terms
of power. Do you want to tell me that the president of
the United States today, be he Democrat or Republican,
sees his function as a person who deals with ideas,
or even ideals, or with fools? We are ruled by pollsters.
Every day there is a poll being conducted somewhere
for the White House, for the government. The pollsters
are the rulers of the country. That's not what we should
have.

**Are you saying, let's just recognize in this country a dichotomy between power and the people, and between the president and the intellectual who deals with possibilities and ideas and ideals? It sounds as though you are doing the separating.**

No. Altogether, we form one society. And of course I hope that we all work for the republic, which is the noblest task of a politician, or of a statesman, or of an intellectual. We all work for the human family. However, within the framework of that family, what is our role? Alexander, who was the greatest king of all, the conqueror of the whole world, took with him a philosopher, Aristotle. Why? What did Aristotle know about politics or about military matters? But he needed him. Even Caligula had someone who asked questions. In the case of dictatorships, of course, they all go to jail or to the guillotine.

But whenever intellectuals get power, it's dangerous. Take the French Revolution—Danton, Robespierre, Marat. They were intellectuals. And because of that they became dictators. The moment they assumed power, it was dangerous for everybody. They became victims of their own experiments. Danton was beheaded, Robespierre was beheaded, Marat was assassinated. Take the Catholic Church. In the beginning, it was a church of ideas, of spirituality. It was a laboratory of the soul. The moment the church acquired power, I think it realized that it was no longer the soul that mattered.

**In the White House in recent years, we have had a large number of scholars—Rhodes scholars, intellectuals. Where would you put your bet—on the intellectual with political**

power or on the politician who draws upon the intellectual? I gather it's the latter.

Right. But still, I would like the intellectual to have access; if not access to power, at least the ear of power. That is the main thing.

**And when the intellectual is given that access to power, what goes with it? In particular, what obligations are there for the politician, the ruler?**

To listen, which is rare. And then to be sure that the intellectuals at his disposal, at his service, should come from opposing sides. The problem is that when the president of the United States goes into the White House, he usually brings the best scholars he knows. As you said, like the Rhodes scholars. Franklin Roosevelt had his Columbia friends. Kennedy had his from Harvard. However, I would like the president to bring in scholars, theoreticians, philosophers, moralists, from both sides, so he always hears two ideas, not one. And then he would know what decision to make.

**I really meant to ask that question in a very different way. Not: What does the political leader give up? But: What does the intellectual give up when involved in politics? What degree of independence of mind is surrendered when one becomes a member of the court?**

That is really the danger. I think that the ruler should need the intellectual. But I hope that the intellectual will not yield to temptation. Because for the intellectual, it's dangerous to be too close to power. There is something in power that corrupts—worse than that, that disturbs, perturbs, disfigures the thought process. I have seen it too much. A person who is close to the ruler changes—

smiles more often, doesn't say things that the president doesn't want to hear. And therefore, slowly, the intellectual becomes the expression of the ruler and the instrument of the ruler, rather than the other way around.

**You say you've seen that happen too often.**

I've seen it, sure. I don't like to go to Washington for that reason. Years ago, when I became the chairman of the first President's Commission on the Holocaust, I saw what Washington does to people. I saw one person who, in a few months, was no longer the same person because of the access to senators and to congressmen and to the White House and to advisors. It's not something I would advise my friends to hope for or to aspire to.

**Does that mean that we in the academy are that weak-minded?**

No, but the seduction of power, the temptation of power, the possibilities of power, are extraordinary. You know, a person in the White House has the cars, the Secret Service. One telephone call and he gets the marvelous jet taking him anywhere. He will also be able to pick up the phone and speak to a Putin or to a Chirac or to a Tony Blair, or to any other world leader. There is something of the aphrodisiac in all of that.

**You have participated in organizing a new group, the Universal Academy of Cultures. Is this a means of channeling intellectual thought, intellectual power, into public life?**

It's to create another forum for intellectuals to analyze, to scrutinize, to specify, what the problems of the day are. I like dialogue. That's my life. I would like to see people, the best-qualified people, by definition, come and discuss a certain subject every year. And if the people in power will listen to us, good. If not, at least we have tried.

**And you will separate those with real power from those with merely intellectual aspirations?**

We don't take any member who is in power.

**You mean that power really precludes one, in your estimation?**

Yes, because it's not the same thing anymore if you have a prime minister or a president. We do have *ex*-presidents.

**So the qualification is being out of power?**

Yes, out of politics and out of power. If I can get bankers or leaders in private industry who are qualified intellectually—most of them are, I hope—they will be taken. Why not? But those in power, that's dangerous. I wouldn't recommend that.

**How will you function? As a Grand Academy?**

We will have seventy members. We already have fifty or so, from all over the world, many Nobel Prize winners and so forth—writers, poets, sociologists, architects. We will work as an academy, this group. We want to give a huge prize every year comparable to the Nobel Prize but covering only the areas the Nobel Prize is not covering.

**To what end?**

To show that the spiritual endeavor, the intellectual process, is part of civilization, and that we offer the same privilege of honoring men and women who do their best to move history one step forward.

**Won't this be a further step toward the elitism that many people see as standing in the wings—that in our times the intellectually rich are getting richer and the poor are getting poorer?**

Richer? Richer in what way? The members of the academy don't get money.

**I meant in terms of those who have had the blessings of education—that those who have been able to avail themselves of the great thoughts of the present and of the past are becoming fewer and fewer, comparatively speaking, and more and more isolated from the community of mankind.**

No, the idea is just the opposite. We have received things that others don't have, it's true—the privilege of studying, the privilege of learning, the privilege of sharing. So what should we do? If we say we don't want to show we are elitist, then we should stay in our residence, in our room, at our desk, and work by ourselves, never to give. But the very fact that we give is humiliating to some. Therefore, many don't want to receive. So should we do that? I believe that because we receive, we must give back. I feel very strongly we must give back, even in America. I am a foreigner here. I came here as a refugee. And I'm grateful to this country. But I always feel I have to give back to it. Therefore, the minorities here, of all shades and classes, I try to the best of my abilities to be of help. I have to give back.

**Eighty years ago, Walter Lippmann, in his great, seminal book *Public Opinion,* wrote about "organized intelligence." He thought there was hope for us only if we could organize the intelligence of the world. Is there some of that in your academy?**

Oh, in moments of grandeur I hope that that is what we achieve. But I am really much more modest. I believe in small things; in touching one person. I don't want to touch millions.

I'll give you an example. We had a conference in Oslo in 1990 and we brought Nelson Mandela, who had just come out of jail, and a minister from the de Klerk government of South Africa. The subject was "The Anatomy of Hate." There were many people—Havel, Mitterrand among them. At one point, the minister from South Africa turned to Mandela and said, "Nelson, I grew up in apartheid. Now my fervent wish is to attend its funeral." And everybody was moved, including Mandela. As a result of that, the dialogue began that ended with the election of Mandela as president. We were in on the beginning of the end of apartheid. Two men who wouldn't have met otherwise, or perhaps only later on, met—because we brought them together. There was something in the air. It worked. I like to be a matchmaker, to bring people together.

**In the beginning there was the word.**

Certainly. What else do we have to give to each other? Money? If we have it, and we can afford it, of course we give it. We should. But what else can we give if not ourselves? And we give it through the word.

**Why?**

Why? Because I'm afraid.

**Afraid?**

I'm afraid of the future. There are so many things that have happened in this world that make me afraid. The violence that is growing daily, including the violence among young people. We have seen thirteen-year-olds become murderers. There is the drug threat. And then, on a larger level, there is what's happening in the world, in Eastern Europe, in the Middle East. We thought democracy would be the answer. It's not, apparently, to my regret and embarrassment. What will happen in India? What about Kashmir? There are so many hot spots, feverish lands, eruptions of ancestral hatreds. I'm afraid of this new century.

**You call it the Universal Academy of Cultures, plural. But didn't we see all around us, at the end of the benighted twentieth century, the conflict between cultures and even their individual representatives? Mustn't one fear these continuing conflicts?**

Yes and no. What we have seen is that one nation—let's say the German nation, the Nazi regime—has tried not to fight another culture but to eradicate it. What did Germany want then? To kill the Jewish people, not only physically, but intellectually, spiritually, metaphysically— to eradicate the Jewish culture, the Jewish memory. I believe in the multifaceted culture. I believe that any culture—a Native American or a Hindu culture—is as good as mine. And we must learn from each other. That is the aim of the academy. That is the aim, I think, of all of us.

**But the concept of diversity seems also to spawn hostility on the part of one culture against another. It's not just a matter of Nazi Germany attempting to eliminate all cultures aside from its own.**

In Russia, with Stalin, of course—

**All right then. But even without these superforces, we now live in an age of conflict between various cultures.**

I don't think so.

**You don't?**

No, I don't think so. We are still in the early stages of

the experiment with history. We are trying to show that each culture must remain sovereign as it opposes other cultures—not to swallow them up, and not to be swallowed by them. But they must remain as they are.

**Do you feel that multiculturalism in this country, and the arrogance, sometimes, of the intellectual in fostering multiculturalism, have led to things you and I do not like, to intolerance itself?**

Yes. One can be tolerant in being against intolerance, you know. I think it was after the French Revolution when they said, "No tolerance for those who are enemies of tolerance." Look, we don't have the absolute answer. There are flaws in every ideology, and there are flaws in every solution. We don't have the solution. I would like for us to at least phrase the questions. What are the questions that dominate our attention, dominate our lives?

**Your job, then, is for your academy to find questions. But don't intellectuals so frequently, in finding questions, feel they must answer them and then push those answers?**

Why do intellectuals continue? Because they have not found the answer. If they found the answer right away, they would stop. But there is something mysterious and beautiful in that—that if I found the answer now, the answer itself becomes a question for tomorrow.

**What do you think your academy will accomplish? What do you want it to achieve over the next fifty years?**

I think, first, I want it to establish a hierarchy of priorities. I would like to introduce, say, morality in science. The scientists should know that there are moral considerations as important as the scientific ones. I would like to bring ethics more forcefully into medicine. All these are issues of life and death, not only for my generation, but for many others as well.

**Do you think your academy will find the means of organizing its intelligence in such a way that you will be able to move these ideas into the public arena?**

Perhaps not. But we'll try.

## INTERLUDE

When I take you out of the mode of asking questions and
put you in the role of prophet—

Oh, no. Prophets ceased to prophesize some twenty-five
hundred years ago. There are no longer prophets. I don't
want to be that.

Well, I know you don't *want* to be.

I'm a student of prophets but not a prophet. I am a student of philosophy, but not a philosopher.

Now, that's not true.

It is true, really. Plato was a philosopher. Spinoza was a
philosopher. Marx was a philosopher. Me, I'm a storyteller.

Many people identified as philosophers have told stories.
But you all tell stories with a point.

Actually, it's with *questions* I am good.

# THREE

# On Being Politically Correct

Political correctness—"PC," as it's known on the campus and off—now challenges Americans who respect and protect others' felt needs and sensitivities, but not at the expense of our freedoms. Elie, I've never met anyone more understanding of and concerned about other individuals' feelings and sensitivities than you are. Does that lead you to sympathy for this politically correct movement?

Not really. I don't like the word "political." If one does what one does because of moral demands, it is one thing. But for political correctness? I don't go for that. I'll give you an example. In my first books, when I wrote in French that the generic *l'homme*—man—does this or that, it meant nothing special to me. I just wrote it. But today, because of the sensitivity of some women, I now say "he or she," or I use the word "person" or "individual," rather than create a kind of antagonism. I made the change to avoid hurting people. I don't like to hurt people. But normally, I simply said, "Man does this,"

"Man is created in God's image." Today, you have to say something else: "God has created man or woman." It's not easy all the time. Sometimes it's difficult to define the proper word and the proper mode in which to say it.

**You say "the proper mode." Isn't that what is being sought by those who are pushing what has, perhaps erroneously, been called PC? It could be morally correct, spiritually correct.**

Morally correct, let's say. The basic idea should be not to humiliate anyone else. I am in favor of that. Why should we humiliate? We're not in the world to humiliate our fellow human beings. But if it's political, I'm against it. If somebody's still using "man," I don't think he should be punished or ostracized for that. We are all free. We can speak the way we want. I have tried to teach the lesson from a different angle. One of my great sources of pride in my class at Boston University is that a student has never been humiliated in my class. Never. If a student says something silly—which happens, of course—instead of laughing, the other students come to his or her defense, and they rally around that person. And it's a good feeling.

**But when I give my seminar at Rutgers, there have been, for the last couple of years, young women who did not register for the class who are seemingly there for the single purpose of saying, "Why are the authors you assign all dead white males?" And I would like to think that they're not being political so much as expressing very human feelings: "We would feel so much better about ourselves if you had picked women to be present on the list." And I wonder whether we don't have some extra obligation to be aware of these feelings.**

I have the same problems, naturally. I go back to the classics and into the antiquity of literature and there is Plato, there is Socrates. But when students come and say, "What about women?" I try to find an answer.

**I'm in the same position. I teach John Stuart Mill, male. Socrates, male—**

Socrates is a male. What can you do? We have to deal with what we have. Nevertheless, I make an effort to find something different. And really, if I do not find enough, at least I focus on the way my students who are young women see the same stories from their viewpoint. I listen to them.

**You and I are, if I may say, wise enough to know that the words we speak do impact others. Isn't there something to this humanly correct movement that must appeal to our consciences?**

There is. Let's say there are black men and women whom you like—who are your students, your peers, your colleagues, your friends. At the beginning, of course, the pejorative word, the shameful word, was "nigger." So nobody uses that word. We should respect that. It shouldn't be used because it was a terrible word. But then came the word "black." Right? Now, I've asked these friends of mine, "What word would you like me to use?" And they say, "Call us African-American." So I call them African-American. Why not? It just requires a little bit of effort in the beginning. Before saying the word "black," you say, "African-American." It's not much to ask, really.

**Now, this is a choice you make. And you make it willingly. What is your position on the efforts being made to enforce—this is particularly true on the campus these**

days—the choice of words, the use of words, and to some extent the use of sources, reading materials?

As a teacher and as a student, I resist force. I resist compulsory orders coming from anywhere. If I want my colleagues to teach certain books, I could go and tell them, without giving orders, "Look, it's important. Understand why." But that is not to say, "If not, you will be punished. You will be ostracized."

Freedom of teaching is the basic element in education. If a teacher doesn't feel free, the teacher is not a good teacher. And therefore the student will lose. They will lose more than the teacher himself. I was at the City College of New York before I went to Boston University. Then came the time of open admissions. And as a result City College was no longer City College, because there were students who didn't know enough to be in college. And they frightened, they threatened, the professors, saying, "If you fail us, we will beat you up." And some of the professors, I think, were afraid of that, or that they would be accused of racism. Who wants to be accused of bigotry? And I found that terrible, because, on the one hand, it was a nice thing to say there are open admissions, that anyone has a right to study. But on the other hand, what is a college? A good college means good students, those who are prepared for it. At the time the mistake was made, those students who wanted to come to City College should, I say, have been given a year and the teachers best equipped to get them ready to enter. I do not believe in terror as a matter of education.

**But you're addressing yourself to one aspect of it, and I wonder how you would approach another—that is, the terror that directs itself toward students who use such words**

as "nigger" or others that you and I would find clearly un-
acceptable.

Objectionable, absolutely.

**What should be the punishment, if you want to use the
word "punishment," for that?**

I must tell you, I have never seen a student, never heard a
student, use these words. If it happened, I would take the
student to my office and I would speak to him or to her
for an hour or two, or three or four, until that student
understood. If not, I'm a poor teacher. I would put the
onus on the teachers then. If I am a teacher, I must be
able to convince my student not to use certain words
that carry such dynamite, such a weight of hatred in
them.

**That's your usual optimism.**

I'm a romantic. You know that.

**You believe in changeability. It's fascinating, though, that
you say that it would be *your* failure if you weren't able to
change someone else's behavior.**

That's not really behavior.

**What is it?**

It's a provocation. Why does a student use that word? To
provoke; to show that he or she is strong enough to resist
the teacher's authority or respect. And then I would
show the student what it really means to have respect, or
even to resist this respect. It's okay to be disrespectful.
It's all right in academic life, in literature. But there are
limits.

**You play the role now of the psychotherapist.**

No. Not really.

**Isn't that what you are saying? You are sort of denying the
notion that you may be dealing with one nasty bit of work**

here in student A or student B, someone you might in another setting characterize as evil.

They are too young for that. But you know, if that student wouldn't listen, I think that student would be in a position where he or she would have to understand that his or her place is not in my class. Because he or she is only doing harm to himself, to herself, to other students. And the other students, they would, I think, so resent his or her presence that that student would have to leave. But it's never happened to me. Never.

**You are very fortunate.**

And if the student says, "I'm not leaving," then he would stay. I would say, "Look, it's in your interest and mine and the other students' to go." But if nevertheless he wants to stay, he stays.

**That raises the question that's coming up on so many campuses about the notion of expelling students.**

Unless the student was really doing something so outrageous, so immoral, that the administration wanted to expel him, I couldn't.

**Words can be weapons. At what point do we say, "You are, by using taunting, negative, hostile language, attacking another person. Your words have become deeds, and deeds can be punished. Out you go"?**

I listen to the victim. If somebody has been called a bad word—a black person, say—and comes and says to me, "Look, I'm insulted," then I listen to that person.

I'll give you an example—the Crown Heights tragedy in Brooklyn, when a young Jew was beaten up and killed. The whole thing was outrageous. It was a scandal. And those people there in Crown Heights—Jews like me—had a demonstration. I came for the demonstration, where they used the word "pogrom." And I think it was not a proper word to use, because if this was a pogrom, a pogrom would be nothing but this. However, how can you not listen to those who were the victims of a brutal attack, like the brother of Yankel Rosenbaum, who was killed? When he describes it as a pogrom, I don't accept the word, but you have to listen. So in the classroom, too, I listen to the victim.

**The Jews in Crown Heights used "pogrom" to describe what was happening to them. Others have used it for, perhaps, political purposes.**

I'm against that, and I say so publicly.

**Words are very precious to you. You listen to the misuse of words. Do you feel some sense of obligation to stop that misuse?**

If I can, of course I stop it. I teach by example. There are certain words I don't use.

**It seems to me that we are using words as weapons more and more. Not necessarily weapons like "nigger" or "kike," but words to distort what is happening in the world around us—spin control. Is this my own pessimism, or is there any way in which you share it?**

There is much pessimism. I share it, too. We must understand that the tragedy of all tragedies, which we call so poorly "Holocaust"—the word is also not proper—began with words. It began with words, with anti-Semitism, with the propaganda.

Hitler predicted what later happened. The world didn't want to listen. There were words invented to describe what they were doing. So therefore something happened to the words. The language itself became corrupt. It destroyed itself from within. There are certain words we cannot use anymore. I met Nelly Sachs, who was a great poetess in Sweden of German-Jewish origin, when I got the Nobel Prize. And she told me something that moved me to tears. She writes poetry in German. There were certain words she said she couldn't use because those words had been used by the killers. At one point she went through such turmoil that she had to be institutionalized. Very few people knew that. There was a kind of detachment between the poet and the language of the poet. And today there is a detachment, an "alienation," à la Brecht, between us and the language that we hear and that we use. Words no longer mean what they are meant to convey.

So of course I agree with you. Whenever we assault language, something will happen to the human psyche. What is language? "Language is a monument," said the philosopher. It is the great monument of civilization. But it's not a building. If you want to study the history of a people, don't go to museums; go to the language of that people. The way terms grew and aged and died and were resurrected. Take a few words, a sentence, and see what happened to that sentence, let's say between the year 1 of the Common Era and now, and you will know everything about people who used that sentence.

**As you look at language around the world, do you find that we here in America are different in terms of what's happening to our language?**

The language is changing. On the one hand, it is becoming very violent. For instance, you say, "Give me a break." What do you mean, "a break"? Why a break? It's violent. Or we say "cut a deal." On the other hand, when you try to describe horrible things, you use other words that are not so terrible, though I'm not sure that's good. You don't want to say a country is poor; you say it's "underprivileged." It's no longer indulging, let's say, in "revolutions," but in "destabilizations." And during the Vietnam War, we used to speak about the "tempo" of the battle, the "orchestration" of the war. These are beautiful words. Which means something happened to language. I think what we say now, the PC, is a result of that destabilization of the language.

**You write in French.**

I write in French. It's the best language in which to express philosophy. Hebrew is different. Hebrew is a condensed language. One word contains ten.

I think that the American language is more concrete than others. It must be applicable. You must figure out something when you use American. That's why journalism is the best in English. It's the best because it's precise. "The Five W's," you know—you don't have it in other languages. Here, the story must be a story that describes exactly when something happened, to whom, for what and so forth. They don't have it in French. That's why the French reportage is so political. The reporter has the ability to express political views. Not so in America, where the story must be objective.

The American nation, on the other hand, is too noisy. It is the noisiest generation we ever had, I think.

**Words, words, words?**

Not even. They don't mean much, but of course people talk. Discourse and debate have become, I think, violent on both sides. Those who advocate, let's say, abortion, have one discourse and those who are against it have another, naturally. And sometimes I hear things that offend me. I hear those in some circles comparing abortion to the Holocaust. That is something unforgivable. What does it mean—that a woman who is choosing abortion is Hitler? Don't do that. There are enough civilized arguments without having recourse to such exaggerated accusations.

**It seems to me, from the perspective of nearly too many years now, that we are shouting much, much, much more than we ever have.**

We don't talk. We shout. We have so many means of communication. And what do we communicate? Never before have so many people spoken that harshly about each other or to each other. The civility is gone; not only the tenderness, but the friendship in discourse. The minute people oppose each other, they become enemies. Maybe language has also been subjected to too many offenses. And we have to start again to teach our contemporaries how to speak. Because when does violence occur? When language stops. When language dies, then violence becomes another language.

## INTERLUDE

THE FIRST QUESTION in the Bible was not asked by man. Logically it should be man asking of God, "Who am I? What am I doing here? Why did you bring me here? Why did you create me?" Not at all. The first question is when Adam flees from God and God asks, "Ayecha?"—"Where are thou?"

There is a marvelous story of a very great Hasidic master, a philosopher, a mystic, who was in jail, and the warden of the jail was a biblical scholar. So the warden came to see the master and said, "Rabbi, I heard you were here. I know you're a great scholar, and you must answer me something. In Genesis I read that God asked, 'Ayecha?' Is it conceivable that God didn't know where Adam was?" And the rabbi answered, "God knew, Adam didn't."

**That's why you ask questions.**

That's why we ask questions.

# FOUR

# The State:
# Its Proper Role in Our Lives

**How would you identify the proper role of the state?**

I would like a state to be a moral state, meaning that it should see to it that a person can be his own person. Meaning, a child should be a child, not with an old person's responsibilities. A mother should be able to be a mother, so she doesn't have to go into the street and do things that she shouldn't do. A father should be a father, not performing a mother's role. The words should then mean something to the citizens of that state. In other words, I would like, in a moral state, people to be human beings—glorified, disciplined, but human beings. And the emphasis is on "human."

**Mustn't the emphasis also be upon participation by the state in many of the activities of individual lives?**

Oh, I believe that the state is here not as an abstraction, but as a real presence, as a framework. Of course, we elect our leaders. But once the leaders are elected, they don't really care about us. I would like the opposite to be true: that once we elect our leaders to lead us, to work for us, that every day they should think about us—not about our vote, but about our welfare.

**You say that at a time when there seems to be such an enormous buildup of resentment of the state as a presence in our lives. You see the state very differently.**

Well, I'm speaking of utopia. In utopia this is what should happen. But we live in reality. I think politics used to be a very noble endeavor. What is politics? To work for the polis, for the city, for the republic. Today, for reasons that perhaps are unfounded, when you say "politician," it has bad connotations: "He's a politician" means he is using his or her power for purposes or for goals that are not laudatory, are not honest. It shouldn't be that way. And probably it isn't always; there are good politicians, too. But there are so many scandals that appear on the front pages of newspapers, on television, that somehow people are worried, surely concerned, and always suspicious.

**You're obviously saying that not just in the utopia that can't be, but in the society that you want to see come into existence, there's got to be that kind of trust.**

There must be trust. That's why we elect those who govern our lives. Without trust, where would we be, and where would they be?

**Then where do we begin now? When we talk about the proper relationship of the state to the individual, don't we have to either fish or cut bait? Don't we have to say, "Look, these are our representatives. We're going to assume that government is benevolent, not malevolent"?**

Again, I believe they, our representatives, should be, and many probably are. But we only know of those who are not because of communication, because of the press. I am not attacking the press. I used to be a journalist. I am on their side. However, I think about the perception that exists among people who read, and all they know is from what they read—or even worse, all they know is from what they see on television. Now, what should they think then? I am much more lenient toward those who try to give their best to help us, to help the common citizen, to help society. Any senator, any congressman, any mayor, could do better in the private sector. They are giving up a lot.

I was at West Point, giving a lecture. I, who come from Eastern Europe, am really still, deep down, the child I used to be, studying in the yeshiva, very pious. And here I am going to speak at West Point, to thousands of cadets. One of them will surely be a general, maybe president. Maybe ten will be generals. And they gave me a marvelous present. They gave me a parade. Forty-five hundred cadets paraded and saluted me. But I was thinking of that. These young men give service to their country. They could go to engineering schools, medical schools, professional schools, and make money. Instead, they want to serve their country. Therefore, I respect them.

The same, really, can be said about many of our senators and congressmen. Some of them are not so good. Some are, let's say, corrupt. It happens. They're human beings. It depends. Everybody is human here. We should aspire to higher levels. But we are human.

**Let's remove ourselves for the moment from the matter of corruption. There are so many people today who say that**

the American tradition is one that can embrace only a very limited government, that the state has very little legitimate reason to enter into our lives. I wonder where your head and your heart are in this matter.

I am, rather, for deep involvement. Again, it's my tradition. The Jewish tradition is that there are laws, 613 commandments. There isn't a single thing that could be outside these commandments. Whatever I do or you do belongs to that body of laws. Now, the law is important in the Jewish tradition. In ancient times, let's say in Rome, an emperor was killed. And Machiavelli said something very beautiful about it. He said, "Poor Septimius Severus—he didn't know that no tyrant has ever succeeded in killing his successor." But they did kill each other. The main reason was to abolish the laws. The moment the emperor died, all the laws were abolished. The new emperor had to issue new laws. Not in the Jewish tradition—the law remained law when David became king. He was a great king, after all, the great king in our history. But when he sinned, the prophet came and admonished him.

So the law *is* important. I would not want the law to be curtailed or watered down. And I feel, if good people sit in the Senate and the House, and of course in the Supreme Court, somehow the system should work. But we maintain the right to criticize. That is the great contribution of the American Constitution: we can criticize. We may say the law is unjust, the law is unfair.

But in our times, we find increasingly there are those who dichotomize the situation and who talk about citizens on the one hand and government on the other.

Usually those who say that are not just citizens; they are

politicians. I remember Ronald Reagan as president; he would still say "they"—"they in Washington." Because it's an efficient gimmick.

**If it's a good gimmick, that means it strikes a chord today.**

It probably always did.

**Well . . . yes, when Franklin Roosevelt ran against Herbert Hoover, it was also "they—those people in Washington." Still, for a long time in my youth, there was such an enormous respect for officialdom.**

Well, I wasn't here, obviously. In the places where I was, in Romania and Hungary, we had no luxury like that to criticize. I am not even sure we had the right to vote. Today, what I am most afraid of in this state of affairs is cynicism. I see it in students. I try to shield them from cynicism, because a cynic is not even evil—somehow it's different, and worse. The cynic is someone who confuses good and evil.

**The cynic confuses good and evil?**

Absolutely. Who is a cynic? He doesn't believe in good, doesn't believe in evil. So for him, good and evil are the same thing. Today, I'm afraid that we are exposing ourselves to cynicism and to cynics. Therefore, we are suspicious of our government. Look, when you read the stories in the media, what else do you find except an excess of certain negative information? What's going on in Washington? One senator is accused of this, another one is indicted for that. Of course, there are only a few. But it hurts. It hurts the system.

**How do you break that cycle? I mean, increasingly in the past generation we have had so much reason for citizens to be cynical about big government. There have been so many**

episodes in which we know we have been lied to about war and peace, about corruption.

Well, today in the media there is a tendency against cover-up, which is good. Above all, if a politician wants my trust, I must know everything about that politician. But even his private life? That disturbs me.

**What disturbs you?**

The revelations of private affairs. I don't want to know that.

**So you don't think private lives should be made public?**

It should not all become sensationalized. It offends me. What a person does in his or her bedroom is really not my affair. However, political decisions are about public conduct, philosophy, ideology, spirituality. I would like to know as much as I can about those who are going to govern our lives. Naturally, you will say one depends on the other.

**Don't you think that?**

Yes, but . . . you know me already. I do not have firm principles on that, because there are exceptions.

**Now, wait a minute. That can't be true. You do have firm principles.**

Yes, but there are exceptions. The principles are there, but we are human beings.

**Well, how are we going to break the cynicism that you see today? One merely needs to listen to one's neighbor or persons passing by on the street to hear, "There go the politicians again."**

Again, I would like the word "respect" to become . . . respectable. Meaning, just as I would like to respect the person who is governing my life, I would like that person to respect my life and my individuality and my personality. And, of course, when I say "I," I mean every citizen in this land.

**But can a public official do that in a nation of more than a quarter of a billion people? Aren't we perhaps past the time, like it or not, when you can find a state in which it is possible? Haven't we come to deal more and more with a leviathan state that is going to pass more and more rules and regulations?**

Dick, I wish I knew the answer, *the* answer, to this question. What should the society be? I know certain parts of it, but I don't know how these parts should become part and parcel of all attitudes toward society, toward life, toward each other.

One thing I do know is that democracy is not working all the time. We see it in Eastern Europe. It doesn't work. It doesn't work in Russia. It doesn't work in the former satellites. Nevertheless, I don't know any other option. I don't know what could replace democracy. It's still not simply the best, but the *only* way for civilized people, for moral people, or for people who want to live with one another. The same is true here. It's not perfect. It means the system of government is not perfect. And our response to that system is not perfect.

**Yes, but you and I, as American citizens, vote.**

Sure.

**And we're either going to vote for those who say, "We believe this state, of necessity, must extend itself more and more into our lives," or we're going to vote for those who say, "The American tradition must be maintained and the American tradition is hands-off government, out of our lives."**

That's not really what preoccupies me. What preoccupies me is simple things. For instance, what should our attitude be toward a stranger, toward the weak, toward the immigrant? Where should we apply our pressure, on whom, for what reason? These are the problems that preoccupy me. But whether the state—the federal government or the state government or local governments—has more right and more ways to interfere in my life, that doesn't matter to me that much.

**Yes, but when you say your concern is with our neighbor or the dispossessed—**

Or the foreigner, or the stranger who comes in, certainly.

**—those decisions are going to be made presumably by us, and then through us by our government. And I guess my question is, Do we want more government? Do you think in terms of a bigger and bigger brother?**

Let me say some things that I think are simple and very clear. I believe a society is measured by its attitude toward the weak, not toward the strong. At the same time, I do know that we live with what we call "conventional lies," and with paradoxes. And our society now is filled with them. We believe, let's say, that we are the only superpower in the world, and yet we don't use that power. Economically, we know that the two nations that provoked the worst war in history, Japan and Germany, have finally become victorious. They won economically—with our help, of course . . . though Japan has its troubles today. This is a paradox.

Furthermore, we know, for instance, that when a person is elected, that person does not have to fulfill his or her promises, which to me is astounding. Here we know that campaign promises are just that: promises, nothing more. We accept that. Why do we accept that? Why do we accept that candidate the next time? Because the American way of life is that campaign promises are not serious. Not serious? Our lives are now filled with paradoxes. I remember when I came here as a journalist in the late fifties. I remember it was very simple. I remember that politics was open, and sex was private. Now it's the opposite. Now sex is open and politics is private. There are all kinds of things like that.

Still, I am proud of our system, by the way. I think America today is still the greatest democracy in the world, with all of its faults, with all of its shortcomings. Where else could a refugee such as myself be sitting with you and talking about history or about philosophy? I know that I can speak up. If something is wrong, I speak up. If the president does something that I don't like, I have spoken out. When Reagan went to Bitburg, I spoke out, and about other affairs, too. Can you imagine me, in Eastern Europe, speaking even to a policeman back there? Forget about speaking to a president!

So, it is an imperfect society. Of course it is. But we should try to make it as decent as possible, knowing we shall never fulfill all of our dream.

# INTERLUDE

―――――――――

THIS MIGHT BE the best story I have, the story of the just man who came to a wicked city. Let's call it Sodom. He came determined to save its inhabitants from sin and punishment. Night and day he walked the streets and markets, protesting against greed and theft, falsehood and indifference. In the beginning, people listened and smiled ironically. Then they stopped listening. He no longer even amused them. The killers went on killing, the wise kept silent as if there were no just man in their midst. One day a child, moved by compassion for the unfortunate teacher, approached him with these words: "Poor stranger, you shout, you scream—don't you see that it is hopeless?"

"Yes, I see," answered the just man.

"Then why do you go on?"

"I'll tell you why. In the beginning, my child, I thought I could change man. Today I know I cannot. But if I still shout today, if I still scream, louder and louder, it is to prevent them from ultimately changing me."

---

# FIVE

# Religion, Politics, . . . and Tolerance

I was brought up to believe that one never talked about religion or politics, even about money. But we can't *not* do that. Your deep concerns for Israel and for your adopted country, the United States—what do those concerns lead you to believe about tolerance, about the proper relationship between church and state, religion and politics? Different for Israel than for the United States?

In both cases, I would say there should be a separation, total separation. It's not good for religion to be involved with politics. It's not good for politics to be involved with religion. Both lose. And the losers usually are the people.

**Why?**

Because the interests are not the same. In religion there is no concept of elections. Nobody is elected. Moses wasn't elected. There was no election campaign for Moses. He didn't want to become a leader. The same thing throughout the ages. A rabbi is not elected; he is ordained. As to politics, we believe in democracy. People

who speak for the community are elected by that community. Therefore, the two don't go together.

**But in a sense, they have to go together, don't they?**

No. Why do they?

**Because if there is to be comity, amity, if there is to be
peace, mustn't the ordained and the elected work hand in
hand?**

Hand in hand, yes. But one should not be dominated by
the other. Which means the politician should not issue
religious rulings, and the religious leader should not give
political advice.

**Well, suppose we accept that. That's not difficult to accept.**

It *is* difficult. There are religious leaders here who do try
to impose their will, and in Israel as well.

**And the other way around?**

No, not really. What do politicians want? One thing:
They want votes. But not to impose their will. Do you
think it's important for a candidate whether I go to synagogue or not? What's important is to get my vote.

**You mean, then, that in this country, for instance, when
there is a dispute among us about issues that can be con-
sidered religious—whether we're talking about abortion
or many, many other issues—in these instances we are not
talking about power? You're saying we are simply talking
about catering to votes?**

No, I think there are religious leaders who mean what
they say.

**No, no, no. I mean political leaders. This is what we have
found in our country?**

Yes, but some political leaders are religious, and therefore when they oppose or support abortion, they speak
not because of their policy, but because of their reli-

gious beliefs. Others simply believe politically, meaning again the polis. They believe that politically they cannot oppose abortion. But when it becomes a political issue per se, I think it's dangerous.

**But if your principle in life is that each decision we make must be made from a moral perspective, how can we separate that? You wouldn't really differentiate religious perception from moral perception, would you?**

No. But look, what is a moral perception in your eyes?

**Tell me. The right thing.**

My feeling is, the moment we say "moral perception," it means to involve the other. It's not what's good for me, but what's good for you.

**The right thing is what is good for others?**

Others. Not for me. Therefore, a political candidate or a religious leader thinking about, let's say, the problem of abortion, which is so important in this country, must think: What does it do to the mother? What does it do to the child, to the people around? And therefore, what I don't like hearing in this debate—and it has become so violent, it is the most explosive issue in the country—is the hostility. There is hate now in the debate. But the debate is a proper one.

**But the debate perhaps focuses our attention on this question of the proper connection between the state and religion. There are those who say that religion has no role in this debate, that it is a governmental decision. "The relationship between a woman and her body" is the way it is put. Can you accept that?**

Not entirely. Because who makes the decision? Do we allow every individual to make a decision for himself or herself? Or is the government the only body capable of making that decision? Or is it the religious group to which he or she belongs that sets the tone? But that is a moral way of considering the issue. When you come to abortion . . . I don't know. Abortion is mainly an issue with the Catholics. And for them, it's a sacred fight. It's a holy war.

**Can you empathize with them?**

Yes and no. I understand, for instance, that some people say, "At the moment of conception, the fetus is a child. One should not be able to get rid of it just like that." On the other hand, I can empathize with the woman who, for her very own reasons, cannot go on with the pregnancy. In spite of her agony, in spite of her pain, in spite of her despair, she cannot. If she wants to go ahead and have an abortion, I have no right to discourage her. I have many discussions with Catholic priests about this because they want me to be in accord with them, and I cannot do that. You see, the problem for me is also the Jewish viewpoint. What is the Talmudic law? It's not that simple.

**It's very direct, I thought, in Jewish law.**

No. As long as the child is in the mother's womb, the mother's health comes first. Once the child is born, it is the child's. One could ask: What if the mother suffers from mental anguish, not from physical danger? It's not that simple. But I'm glad it's not that simple in Talmudic law, to make sure that everything is taken into account. There should be agony before a person makes such a decision.

**Let me turn for a moment to Israel. How is the answer**

given there to the question we have put to ourselves: What is the proper relationship between religion and the state, religion and politics?

Well, religion in Israel, because of its history, has, unfortunately, too much influence. Religions mix too much in politics, and I don't like that.

**But you're a man of belief, a man of religion, are you not?**

I don't speak about my religion, but yes, I am. I go to synagogue, and my upbringing was such that I continue to believe. But decisions in religious matters belong to religious leaders, meaning to the rabbis.

**And the rabbis and their relationship to government?**

It depends on the time. In our history, there are three categories: the king, the prophet, and the priest. And they were always distinct. They all had their prerogatives. And they somehow never had the role or the right to dominate the others. The priest was the priest in the temple. The prophet was the prophet everywhere. And the king was in his royal palace, conducting the daily affairs of the nation. Today, it's different. Today, because the temple does not exist anymore, we have recourse to other expressions of our attachment to God and his law.

**More satisfactory?**

Never satisfactory, but we try to find a way. I was very religious when I was a child and an adolescent. Very religious. I am not the same now. Of course not. How can one be after what we have witnessed? I speak now about a wounded faith. The faith is there, but wounded.

**One usually heals wounds, or tries to.**

I don't think this wound can be healed. If there were a way to heal it, I would reject it.

**I've never understood this. Is this Wiesel the historian, not Wiesel the theologian?**

I am neither historian nor theologian. I am only a student of history and theology, but I am not an expert in either field. And I am not against paradoxes. You know that. I accept them. It's true, I was terribly religious. I was totally religious. There was nothing but my religiosity that counted at that time. And faith—I can't live without faith now, either. But I don't want that faith to be as pure as before, having gone through what I did go through. So I don't know what to say. I don't know.

**Can we, with integrity and honesty, keep separate moral and religious beliefs as they inform political beliefs? I don't mean postures or posturing.**

We are trying to do that here in the United States, and also in France. Not in Israel, because Israel is still kind of a theocratic nation. But I feel religious people who are sincerely religious—for them, religion means morality—cannot avoid combining the two. And they should not. But then we should tell these religious leaders that morality also means to accept the morality of the other person, if the other person is religious but not the same way that they are. The other person, say, belongs to a different religion; it is also possible he has no religion at all. The morality as such must be above religious morality.

Now, that's not so easy for religious leaders to accept, because for them religious morality means universal morality. What does it mean for the Jew, let's say, who believes in the Jewish cause, in the Jewish religion, in the Jewish faith, in the Jewish law? That only the Jewish law should prevail all over the world? Nonsense. Of course not. We believe one faith is good for the Jews. And other laws are good for non-Jews—for the gentiles, for the Christians, for the Muslims, or for the atheists. Once we accept that, I think, we are already on the way toward a kind of modus vivendi that will prevent religion from becoming a permanent block in a country where obviously, and for good reason, all the people are not of the same religion.

**Yet we have spoken over the years of the point that you made earlier on—that everything we do must be judged from a moral perspective. How do we make those positions jibe?**

Again, by accepting that what I believe to be my need for morality and my quest for ethical considerations must be matched by somebody else's. The problem, of course, is, if they are in conflict, what should prevail? For society, for civilization, it's a kind of adjustment. The moment we say there is no absolute—and that's what I say, there is no absolute—we deal with two attitudes, two attitudes toward culture, toward humanity, that must be matched and adjusted to each other.

**When you look ahead, what do you think is going to happen in this area in Israel?**

I don't know, because things are so unpredictable there. But I think eventually there will be peace with the Palestinians. I think there will be a Palestinian state, recognized by Israel.

What worries me is that religion is on the rise in its most fanatic form. That is true of every religion. We don't even know about certain areas of the world. In the former Soviet Union there are two former republics—Azerbaijan and Uzbekistan—with 70 million Muslims, and they are all moving toward extremism. Then there are two billion Muslims in the world dominated by fundamentalists. The same thing in Israel—it's the fanatic. It's more vocal, and therefore it's terribly dangerous. For the moment, what has happened in Israel is not very nice. I don't like it. I think that the extremists have too much power.

**Why, do you think? You seem to imply that with the . . . strange word—the resolution?—of Palestine, the religious extremists will lose their power in Israel.**

They will lose much of their power. I'll give you an example. Shas is a very religious organization. It's the third-largest party in the Knesset. The Shas party says, "If you give money for our schools, we will vote the way you want us to vote." Which to me is unheard of, to do it so openly. Now, that happens all over the world in parliamentary circles—"If you vote for me, I'll vote for you. You vote for a dam there, I'll vote for your highway here." But at least they do it behind the scenes. There, in Israel, they do it openly, with no shame, no embarrassment. And they say, "For two or three million dollars, go ahead—we'll vote to give back the Golan." Look at what we are doing.

But once the Palestinian issue is resolved, because after all this is the most important issue, I think this will go away. And especially if you manage to keep this state in peace. My advice has been for years, since Oslo, that the president of the United States be a matchmaker. What he needs to do is to say to whoever the prime minister is, and Arafat, or whoever his successor is, "Gentlemen, you must take an oath. For twenty years, you don't mention two items: refugees and Jerusalem. Give cooperation a chance, give peace a chance. And the only way it has a chance is not to mention those two items. Because if they are mentioned, it's finished." I don't know. I hope they will listen to me.

**From a moral perspective, how can you possibly not mention refugees?**

If I do, why shouldn't we mention, then, the three million Germans who were expelled from the Czech Republic in 1945? How can anyone suggest that they all go back to the Sudeten? It's impossible. How about Pakistan and India? Would anyone mention bringing those people back? It would be a tragedy—a result, really, of the first tragedy. I don't like to compare sufferings, but what about the Jews who were expelled from Arab countries? Once you start comparing tragedies, it's a problem.

**You want to make this ground zero.**

Not only that, but also to say, "Give our children a chance that will enable them to do good for the two communities, to bring them closer together." That could mean that Jewish teachers, say, should teach in Palestinian schools, and Palestinian children should come to Jewish schools. And slowly—from kindergarten on—they would start moving closer. For instance, I've heard about pedagogical systems where the class is divided, arbitrarily, into two, for one week. One half is "white" and the other half is "black." One week all the violence and all the bitterness is directed against half of them. They feel as victims. And the next week it is the opposite—the others feel as victims. I would follow the same path. I would use any method to bring the Palestinians and Israelis together.

**Let me come back to the question of the Orthodox in**

Israel. You're almost assuming that the essential, perhaps the only, question there, in terms of their power, is that of the Arab neighbors. Isn't there a demand that stays alive within Israel itself for a theocratic state?

Of course, you are absolutely right. The real problem with Israel is not with the neighbors, it's with herself. But we've lived like that for three thousand years. Sometimes it produced tragedy. Whenever there was a tragedy it was because of internal dissension, as with the destruction of the second temple.

What worries me—I don't even know how to deal with it, because it's too painful—is that I was in Israel on the day when Barak withdrew from Lebanon, the first day. I'd just arrived. And Israel was suffering from shame. You heard that word, "shame": "We are ashamed, we are ashamed, we are ashamed, to leave our comrades in arms behind." And you saw the pictures on television, of the families who had come to the border. The next day it changed, because you saw the South Lebanese soldiers and their families taken care of by Israelis. But the first day was terrible. What worries me is the hatred between Jews and Jews.

I hear that, and have for a dozen years, from everyone I know who comes back from Israel.

I've seen it. Jews hate Jews. Meaning the rich hate the poor, the poor hate the rich, and the—

The hatred among the Jews, you're saying, is also class—

Some people hate because they're rich, others because they're poor. Some because they are white, others because they are not. Some because they are on the right or left. Orthodox against Orthodox. Orthodox against other believers—not even against agnostics. It never happened before. For the first time, at least in our modern history, the various splits are so deep.

**You must have some sense of why this is happening.**

Maybe because history is moving too fast and it brings everything up from the depth of our collective psyche, whatever happened thousands of years ago.

**Is there any effort in Israel to examine this question of hate?**

I hope so, but you know, I don't live there, I've never lived in Israel, so I didn't dare to ask. Close friends have mentioned this to me, too, and they ask what I'm doing about it. I said, "Let's wait until things quiet down on the borders." It was an excuse, a pretext.

**There's never been any time in history where there was a parallel, similar—**

Again, the destruction of the second temple was internally led.

**And why?**

You can almost use the same vocabulary, because the extremists fought the middle. There was always someone to fight against. They fought harder against each other than they did against the Romans who besieged Jerusalem. There was a group called the Sicarii—named for the dagger that they kept under their clothes—and they would attack the Romans from behind. And if the Romans didn't attack, they attacked each other.

**I came here to feel better.**

Now you feel better. Because, after all, this happened two thousand years ago, and we are still here. What happened to the Roman Empire?

**What have been the changes over the years that you have felt about yourself in your thinking in this regard?**

First of all, what I mentioned earlier—my religious life. The thirst is there, the quest is there, but the wound had not been there before, and now it is. And also my attitude toward non-Jews changed.

**How?**

When I was in my little town as a child, I couldn't imagine myself being the friend of a priest. It was impossible. To see somebody with a cross . . . a cross for me was a symbol of torment, not of love. I never knew what was going on in a church. There was a church on my street, and I would cross to the other side because I was afraid of something, I didn't even know what—that I would be kidnapped or converted by force or something. I was afraid, so I changed sidewalks. I was right then, but I would be wrong if I did it now. I was convinced that whatever I knew about Christianity was that Christians hated Jews.

But I learned something—that I must not pass judgment. There are good Christians and bad Christians, just as there are good people and there are bad people. So I have friendships. The cardinal of Paris is one of my closest friends. A former cardinal of New York was another good friend of mine. I know many priests, many serious, sincere Catholic and Protestant thinkers, and Buddhist thinkers and Muslim thinkers. I have no right to close my world and say, "This is my world, and the other world doesn't exist." I am open to those who are open to my world.

**When we first met a couple of decades ago, I think you would have said the same thing.**

Not as much, no. I'll give you an example: the pope. I was terribly suspicious of this pope at the beginning because of what he did when he became pope, when he went to Auschwitz. It was good that he went to Auschwitz, after all, but what did he do in Auschwitz? First of all, he only invoked two names. One was Edith Stein, the Jewish convert. And the other was Maksymilian Kolbe, who was an anti-Semitic priest. These two became symbols. Number two, in all his homilies he never mentioned the word "Jew." To be in Auschwitz and not to mention the word "Jew"—one really has to make an effort to do that. Worse, he celebrated a mass for the victims in Auschwitz and I felt, "My God, 99 percent of the victims here are Jews, most of them from Hungary." And instead of calling on a rabbi and saying, "You say Kaddish for the Jewish victims and I will celebrate mass for the others," he didn't. He simply celebrated the mass. He wanted to convert them posthumously. So I was terribly upset. And then, later on, there was the way he behaved toward Kurt Waldheim. He was too close to the Austrian chancellor. And at that time he was also one of the first to receive Arafat.

Now I must tell you that I have learned to respect and admire and have affection for him. After all, he organized a concert commemorating the Holocaust in the Vatican. He went to synagogue in Rome. He recognized Israel, and handled himself well in Israel after that. He had changed.

**And you?**

I think both of us changed. You know, we were supposed to meet. After he met Waldheim, there was such an uproar that five cardinals whom I knew wanted me to go and see the pope, telling me he had read my books and wanted to meet me. I said no at the beginning, because I felt it was a manipulation. He would say, or at least his people would say, "The pope sees everybody. He saw Waldheim, and he sees Wiesel. Why not?" I said no, and that went on and on. Finally his secretary of state came to see me, and we met in a secret place because I didn't want the press to interfere. And it was just, "The Holy Father wants to see you." And I said, "I don't think this is the proper time for it." Finally, I set certain conditions: the meeting would not be an audience, but a disputation, in the real sense, not limited in time. The main thing was secrecy—no leaks, with no one present.

That happened in June 1987. We were supposed to meet in August. Everything was ready. That summer, I did nothing else but prepare myself for that meeting. I knew everything that went on in Jewish history, between Jews and Christians, from the beginning. Every letter, every discussion, I knew it. But my visit was to be a secret. Then one day in early August I came back from Brazil—I had to be there for twenty-four hours—and when I landed in New York, I bought the *New York Times* at the airport, and there it was, a big story: "Wiesel is going to see the pope." So I canceled. By the time I came from the airport, you can't imagine what was going on. Everybody was going crazy. Many journalists wanted to be there. It was going to be a circus. But I didn't want a circus.

Anyway, I maintained my reservations about the pope. But he changed. And I changed.

**And the disputation?**

The disputation remains on the table. But he's aged. He's not what he used to be.

**That is a major change.**

Absolutely. But it also means Jews leaning toward a rap-
prochement with Christianity. Jews now have a lot of
meetings with Christians, and theologians often meet
and work together. But I wish they would include Muslims.

**That hasn't happened yet.**

Not yet, but I think we should bring in the Muslims
too—bring the three monotheistic religions together and
do it with respect for each. It all goes toward what we
said earlier, to deprive religion of its nefarious possibilities in human relations.

## INTERLUDE

You say you are not political, but moral, in your outlook.
How proper is it for a moral spokesman to pronounce individual judgments upon issues that come before us in a
political way?

It's easy. Those who make a right judgment are good
for me; those who make a wrong judgment are wrong
for me.

Do you have sympathy for those who would say that Wiesel
should stay away from those issues?

Not at all. I think quite the opposite. I think moral
spokesmen should introduce their concerns into the political field. Otherwise you will have politics without
outsiders, without nonpoliticians. I would like to be able
to speak up. I would like to quote Shakespeare, Dostoevsky, Tolstoy . . . why not? Why not elevate the debate?
Why not elevate the whole discourse?

In the political mix, when the result—even though based

on majority rule—does not point in a moral direction, what position must we take?

Oh, I think that we who are, after all, teachers, writers, philosophers, artists, should always have the courage to speak up. Who is a writer? Someone who can say no to the system, no to the surroundings, sometimes even no to God.

**Someone who believes there is a higher law?**

At least a higher voice. That means a writer may say, "No, I don't accept this or that." And because I am a writer and because I am a teacher, I may say, "I don't accept the way things are running." I know it doesn't make much sense, because who am I to say to presidents, to vice presidents, or to senators how to run a country? I know nothing about it. But although I don't know anything about it, I have the right—even the moral obligation—to say I don't like it.

# SIX

# Nationalism and Upheaval

You received the Nobel Peace Prize for your lifelong efforts at achieving peace among men and women and between nations. But even as you have devoted its rewards to furthering your dissection of the anatomy of hate, the face of the world has changed. How are the dramatic national upheavals we experienced lately likely to impact upon your efforts?

It's not easy. The events are too many, and they go fast, too fast. You don't have time to catch your breath, literally. Who would have thought that the Communist empire would crumble in three days? What happened to Lenin? What happened to Stalin? What happened to the terrifying leaders of Soviet Russia? What happened to their disciples, to their teaching?

I was in Russia during the putsch. I met Gorbachev. I can tell you, I saw the loneliest man in the world. I have rarely seen a man as lonely. All of a sudden, I tried to imagine him as a novelist would. If I were to write a novel, he would belong to Dostoevsky, to Pushkin, to Tolstoy. All this, actually, was a novel, a huge, dramatic novel. And he was there and I imagined what he was thinking. I felt he must have thought, My God, I believed in friendship. After all, communism is comradely friendship. All of his friends betrayed him. He believed in communism. That was his life, that was his faith . . . and it crumbled. He believed in power; he was one of the two most powerful men in the world . . . and he had no power. The power that he had, he received from Yeltsin, who wasn't his friend, or from a few security guards who stayed loyal to him. But what did he think? He was sad. He looked so melancholy because he was alone, and I'm convinced that when he came out from his prison, he must have seen that something went wrong with history in his land, and therefore with the psyche of people he had known.

What went wrong? The fact is that it collapsed from inside. It is not the Western world that defeated the Communist empire. It was defeated by itself. So what were the forces here, the forces of evil that all of a sudden gave in, and to whom, to what? Now we're thinking about it and I must say I am not entirely at peace with what is happening. I'm worried.

**Why?**

First, because of the pace. I'm glad that it happened, of course. When nations regain their right to be sovereign, to be free, it's beautiful. I use the word advisedly. We need beauty, and there is beauty in that victory. But I'm afraid of what comes after. What will replace communism? Communism, after all, was a movement that inspired hundreds of millions of men and women all over the world. Now they are left empty—empty of faith, empty of ideas, empty of ideals. What can replace communism? Will it be religion? Because after all we must also recognize that together with communism, atheism has abdicated. You should see in Russia the return to religion everywhere—Christian, Jewish, Muslim; the young people coming back to religion. Will religion succeed communism? Maybe it will be nationalism as well. If so, it's dangerous, because religious nationalism is very dangerous.

**How do you, a religious person, view the rise of religion?**

I feel religion must be a humanizing experience. If religion becomes a tool in the hands of a fanatic, then it is bad religion and that fanatic betrays God, just as he or she betrays people. And unfortunately, fanaticism and religion have gone hand in hand for too long. I'm afraid of that. Once you believe that whatever you do you do in the name of a higher power, that you do it for the sake of God, it's dangerous. And I would like to believe that as a Jew, I am what I am. And I respect those who are not Jewish. As somebody who does come from a religious background, I have tried to define myself from within that tradition, but I respect anyone who does not belong to that tradition, as long as that spirit of tolerance is shared. I don't want to be faced with intolerance, for that I have to answer a different way.

**In an intolerant way?**

I don't know, but I know I cannot be tolerant to the intolerant.

**One used to think of you as one who would be tolerant to the intolerant.**

I think I would fight intolerance with words, I wouldn't

use force. I don't know how. I don't want to use weapons. But I would fight it with language, surely. Intolerance in any way, under any disguise, is wrong. Not only for me, but for anyone. We cannot admit that intolerance should have the last word, except, that is, in the service of tolerance. And intolerance is never in the service of anyone except the fanatic.

**Do you think those who stood on the sidelines and cheered, for a few years, "the end of history" have been unrealistic about the rise of nationalism and of religion as you describe it?**

No, because we are dreamers, and I think it's good to dream such dreams—that it's possible to overthrow dictatorship. But it is maybe a source of anguish, or should be, that we had not foreseen this. No one had. The CIA had not, the KGB had not, the Mossad in Israel had not, the French Deuxième Bureau had not. It all came as a surprise. So much so that I would suggest doing away with all of these intelligence agencies. What we need is to take the budgets for all this intelligence work and build more schools, more hospitals, more institutions to help children simply grow up as decent human beings.

**What do you think is going to be the impact of the rise again of nation-states—no longer the Soviet giants but rather individual states, feeling their oats?**

Every week another nation is born. Monaco is now a member of the United Nations—a nice, beautiful little city with a small police force. It's a pleasure to go, you know, to sunlit Monaco. But to become a member means that Monaco now has the same vote as the United States or England. It's okay. It doesn't bother me. What bothers me is when a nation becomes so nationalistic that it infringes on the sovereignty of another nation. What will happen to Armenia and Azerbaijan? Will they now live in peace, because they will be free? Can you guarantee that there is no madman among the colonels or the sergeants in Armenia, or in Azerbaijan, who may have access to some nuclear missiles? You think they won't use them against each other? That's my real worry—that hatred in this case could produce a world disaster, because once unleashed the nuclear evil will dominate history to come. I never compare anything to Auschwitz, but I think Auschwitz paved the way for Hiroshima.

**As a response?**

Not as a response; as a possibility. It's possible to kill a community of people. Today, there are so many nuclear weapons, and fortunately, for the moment, the big powers, I think, are responsible. They won't use them. But one day, smaller nations will get hold of them, and we know they will use them. What then?

**What would you do?**

I don't know. I don't know all the details. I don't read the secret intelligence reports every morning. I don't know what armies we have. I don't even know what it means to be a soldier. But I would establish a UN policy that would police, first of all, the nuclear area. I am terribly worried about the nuclear implications. Today there are at least three republics that belonged to the former USSR that are nuclear. Now, the conditions there are known. A captain, I think, makes thirty dollars a month, if not less. There must be among those captains or lieutenants or majors some people who are corruptible. Imagine a Khadafy, a Saddam Hussein, sending emissaries to corrupt them and offer one general a hundred thousand dollars or more and a visa to Switzerland. Nuclear weapons could be stolen. So I would like to have international police under the UN to see to it that such proliferation does not occur.

**At the end of the Second World War there was a tremendous enthusiasm for the multiplicity of ethnic and national groups that would now have their own voice, their own power. There was empowerment there. How has it led to chaos and warfare today?**

Well, even in 1945 there was a kind of urge not only to be free, but to be free within a universal society. Logically, we should have decided then that nationalism was the wrong path, because it had led toward Nazism and Fascism. But the opposite occurred. You had many colonies that wanted to be free. Israel became a sovereign state. India became independent as a nation. So fifty years later, where are we? We see a disintegration of moral values. Something went wrong.

**Went wrong, or is there something inherently wrong about the concept of separateness?**

Well, that's the beauty of the human being. I am I. Am I alone? I am I only because you will also say the same thing about yourself. If I respect your individuality, then I would hope that mine, too, would also be respected. The same should apply to a community. If a community is respected, I think, it will respect others. However, what we see now in Eastern Europe especially, or in Bangladesh, India, Pakistan, is that the respect for someone else's liberty, or national identity, is gone. So again, something went wrong.

**Has there ever been a time when indeed that emphasis hasn't led to this group against that group?**

Yes and no. Since the beginning of human history, there were wars—tribal wars, religious wars, national wars. Geographical considerations entered into the play, of course. But what did it mean? It meant that one community felt it was superior. The moment that happens, then something is wrong. When wars occurred between nations, it was because one nation wanted conquest. Why did it want to conquer the other? Because it felt that it had the right for its citizens to have better conditions, more money, more food, more power. Usually, when religious wars occurred, it was because one religion felt that only its members had God's ear, so to speak—that only they could interpret God's word. And those religious wars were vicious, brutal, cruel, murderous.

So what went wrong now? We feel that the question of democracy is really at the heart of the problem. We offer countries democracy, or they got democracy. And why did it go wrong?

**Why did it go wrong?**

I wish I knew. Ask those countries. Superficially, we do get answers. But what are the answers? The Serbian spokesmen say that we were wrong in the United States and in Western Europe to recognize the sovereignty of Croatia or of Bosnia right away. But these are just cover words. What went wrong, I think, is that hate continued to exist and to do damage to the soul of the people. Hate was not disarmed.

**If we continue to foster, in the name of individual freedom**

or nationalism, the notion of sovereignty for this group or that group, aren't we bound to rekindle all the old hatreds?

Not necessarily. Take France and Germany. They were enemies, and in terrible wars. France and Germany, for a few hundred kilometers, would kill tens of thousands of people. And yet today they are linked together and they are ready, within the framework of the European community, to give up many components of sovereignty. You can go from France into Germany without a passport. So it's possible.

**How do you explain what happened there? Something you wouldn't have expected at the end of the First World War or the Second World War.**

At the end of the Second World War it was simple, because Germany was defeated and the others were the victors. In 1945 there was a utopian feeling that this was the last war—no more wars. Surely not a war with Germany, because Germany would not have the strength to start one again. We had the feeling here and in France that the demons were killed. There was no more thirst for conquest in Germany, because Germany itself had seen what it had done in the name of conquest, in the name of power, in the name of nationalism.

**Do you feel as sanguine as the French do about the future of Germany?**

Oh, I am afraid of what's happening in Germany. I belong to a certain traumatized generation. For me, whatever happens in Germany takes on a different meaning. It doesn't mean I condemn the entire German people. I do not believe in collective guilt. Nobody should say that a people is guilty. Strangely enough, the Bible speaks about a sinful city that should be burned with everything in it. And yet Talmudic commentaries make it their business to say that such a city never existed and never will. So the law is the law. You cannot say a community, a people, all together, are guilty. There is no such thing.

**You use that telling phrase "a traumatized generation." Two things occur to me: One is that it is an explanation for your rejection of this biblical injunction. On the other hand, you are part of a traumatized generation that obviously doesn't fully share in the terms of your emotions.**

I still believe we cannot condemn the entire German people. First of all, there are those who were born after the war or during the war. And some of them were my students or are my students, and they are the best that you can imagine. They are the ones who went back to Germany to organize the candlelight demonstrations against xenophobia, against racism.

But why am I nevertheless so concerned with Germany? Because why should there be young people in Germany today—skinheads, Nazis, neo-Nazis—who walk and parade in the streets of certain cities and openly spread hate? Don't they know? I would somehow understand this of a seventy-year-old German who used to be a colonel in the SS, that he should think with melancholy or nostalgia of the Hitler years. In his mind it makes sense. After all, those were the best years of his life: He could kill with impunity, rob with impunity, rape with impunity. He was king. But the young people? Why should they go for it?

**You'll forgive me, but it seems that question, the question of innocence, reflects your continuing notion that anywhere, at any time, it might be possible to find no hate.**

After all, we have skinheads in our own country. So it's not a function of Germany.

Here it's less meaningful, so to speak.

Why?

Because we were spared that experience. In Germany it means something. It's Treblinka, it's Auschwitz, it's Bergen-Belsen. Here we don't have that evil. Here, at least, we know, on the contrary, that we fought it. Look, I am critical of Roosevelt for not having done enough to save the Jews. But nevertheless, he was a commander-in-chief who went to war to save the world. And he did it with resolve and fortitude. So we should know that part. But why shouldn't German young people know their part?

You're looking to an image of humanity that makes skinheads something outside the framework of human nature.

No. No, I do not say that. I think there is something of the skinhead in every one of us. Now, I don't say that there is an Eichmann in every one of us. Only Eichmann was Eichmann. And only the Nazis were Nazis. I don't believe there is a Nazi in every person. Because it's like saying every person is a potential killer. Unless I kill, I am not a killer—not even a potential killer. The choice is mine. We have to choose to be a friend of humanity or a foe. The skinheads have chosen to be foes of humanity. So we must, with our ways and tools, create the right climate in this country. But to be a skinhead, a person who is a vehicle of hate, is a foe of whatever human beings aim to achieve.

Why don't we look at the phenomenon of hate in another part of the world: How are we going to deal with the exchange of hatred between Israel and its surrounding national enemies? Let's start with the question of whether the Palestinians have a right to have their own national identity.

Yes. In Israel, many say there is no need for another Arab nation. That is a problem to be dealt with within Israel. What I would say is to create the Jordanian Kingdom of Palestine, so the word "Palestine" will be part of the name of that country. Which means the Palestinians would have their own passport, from the Jordanian Kingdom of Palestine, which would be Jordan and part of the territories. I think if that can be achieved, that should be a kind of basic formula on which to work and to search for more possibilities, more options. I think that could be a good way to begin.

We see now that ancient hatreds surface and are extraordinary in the intensity with which they burn. Do you think the ancient hatreds will disappear with a new nation?

Oh, sure. That is not so ancient. Palestinians? Fifty years ago Jews were Palestinians. There was a Jewish Agency for Palestine, the Jewish Brigade for Palestine, and that meant Jewish Palestine. "Palestinian" became a word carrying hostility toward the Jews much later.

We are dealing now with two or three generations of conflict.

That may be so. The moment they have something of a national territory, national identity, then they will have to cooperate with Israel.

What has happened to the phenomenon of anti-Semitism in Eastern Europe?

Anti-Semitism is there. Therefore hatred is there. I don't believe that anti-Semitism can be a limited phenomenon. Those who hate Jews hate other people as well. Those who hate Jews hate blacks, hate Muslims, hate minorities . . . they always find other people to hate. In Poland there's anti-Semitism without Jews. I was in Romania during the fiftieth anniversary of the pogrom. You find there two weekly newspapers, with a tremendous circulation, that are openly, viciously, outrageously anti-Semitic. I asked the president, I asked the prime minister, I asked writers, colleagues of mine and yours, "Why are you silent?" And they said, "We are afraid." I said, "Why don't you publish articles, at least, say something, sign petitions?" After the visit, they did sign petitions. The fact is, I'm sure it's the result of what happened in Washington. The Senate and the House of Representatives unanimously adopted resolutions condemning anti-Semitism in Romania, and calling upon the President to tie economic aid to the efforts of the government to fight anti-Semitism.

In Russia there is Pamyat. Pamyat is a vicious group. Around Pamyat exists a periphery of anti-Semites. And these people openly say they want to kill Jews. They simply say they don't even want the Jews to go to Israel, because they want to deal with them in Russia.

**To what extent did the totalitarian states in Eastern Europe, over the past several decades, diminish the impact of this anti-Semitism?**

Because they diminished freedom of speech, and since nobody spoke, the anti-Semites couldn't speak either, unless the government wanted to be anti-Semitic, which you remember in Stalin's time. When Stalin became anti-Semitic, the entire Communist empire became officially anti-Semitic. The Jews were not free, and the enemies of the Jews were not free, either. But once freedom came, Eastern Europeans used it and they abused it.

**It's strange to think of such activities—mental, physical, or otherwise—as part of the uses of freedom.**

That is, of course, the price we pay for democracy, and I'm not sure what to do about it. But what is the alternative? I would not suppress the freedom of speech, I would not suppress the freedom of expression, I would not suppress the freedom of belief.

**Why wouldn't you? When you have as great an evil as you have witnessed, why would you not prohibit it?**

Because I still believe in the power of the word and the power of the mind and the power of language and the power of argument, and I think that those who fight anti-Semitism or racial hatred are intellectually strong enough and should be morally strong enough to defeat the anti-Semites without resorting to the law.

**You hope or you believe?**

Both. I'm divided—my heart and my mind. Rationally, I think I'm wrong. I'd rather have laws against it. In some countries, there are laws. Incitement against people is illegal in France, for instance. It should be here, too. But deep down I prefer to think that because we are teachers and because we know how to use ideas, the ideas of humanity are stronger than the temptations, the seduction, of inhumanity.

**Are we ever going to solve these problems until less sovereignty resides in individual nations and more in world councils themselves?**

If we could create a world federation, it would be utopian. But you know, the word "utopian" means, in so many words, "It never happened. It never existed. It doesn't exist." I would say it was "messianic." But even when the Messiah comes, it wouldn't mean the abolition of messianism. It would simply mean that all nations would have respect for one another.

**You see that city on the hill? You see it coming?**

Oh, I hope it will come. I don't see it. But I see it must come one day. As a Jew, I believe it must come.

**And through what agency?**

It must be a human endeavor, not a divine endeavor. It is we who can make it happen, if even for a year. Maybe it won't last eternally. But if we can do it for one year, it would be worthwhile.

**What feeds your hopefulness?**

Oh, it's absurd.

**Your hopefulness is?**

Naturally. But I try to nourish it, to feed it and then to strengthen it. I believe there are mystical forces in history, irrational forces. We should try to understand them, to explore them, to evaluate their strength. I mean, there are so many events taking place in our lifetime that I have the feeling we are living in biblical times. There is a script somewhere. Maybe. What is the script? Who has written it? Can we read it? Who is decoding it?

**You see some mysterious hand. You call it a script.**

At least let us say there is a mystery there. Now, I don't know who the author of that mystery is. If I'm a believer, I would say, of course, it's God. If not, I would say it's destiny. But we are forced more and more to confront that mystery.

**And the meaning of the script that has been written?**

Oh, to me the message is clear. The message is that we

are coming closer and closer to the brink, to the abyss. We know that the abyss is there. For the first time we have that knowledge. That means we know that it is enough now for one superpower to make a mistake and we will be in the abyss

**Well, how have you reacted to the notion of the end of history?**

You know, I am a Jew, and I study Jewish sources, and when I hear an expression like this, I go back to my sources. In mysticism, you read about "the end of times." We don't say "end of history"; there is no word for "history" in Hebrew, in biblical language. But for us the end of times is not an apocalyptic event, it's a redemptive event. That means we're close to redemption. And when we say the end of times is coming, that means redemption is here.

**Isn't that in a sense what "the end of history" has been taken to mean?**

I think the end of history means many things to many people. It can also mean that there is nothing else to do.

**You mean a shrug of the shoulders?**

Exactly. There's nothing else to do, it's the end of history. What is history? History, after all, is an experiment, a laboratory. And it is given to us so we can work in it and on it and on ourselves. I know that when I work on myself something is happening to someone else, rather than working on someone else and forcing him or her to do things that I want.

I'll tell you, I once had the feeling that the world had come to an end, and that was in 1944. The darkest moment of my life. That night I had the feeling of the end of history, the end of times—and the end of the Jewish people. I saw people coming from all over history, from all over the world, all over the Diaspora, speaking all languages, representing all areas of human endeavor, young, old, rich, poor, ignorant, learned, all of them. I figured they were drawn to the fire. And my feeling was, This is the end. It was. The world had come to an end then. But it is given to man to build on the end, to build on ruins. What else can we do?

**What is there for us to have learned from the strange, strange twentieth century?**

The story.

**You are always the storyteller.**

It's a very beautiful Hasidic story. Two men meet by accident. The first is alone in the forest, lost. He doesn't know the way out. A day passes. He is in panic. Then he sees the other man. And he's so happy. He runs to him and says, "Thank God that you are here. Now, please show me the way out." And the other one says, "Look, I'm also lost. All I can tell you is, don't go this way. I just came from there." This is the story—this century we should learn not to go back to the twentieth century.

**Why has it been such a horrendous period in man's history?**

Maybe every century seems horrendous and filled with fear and anguish. But ours, really, I think, crossed a threshold. The past century was the most violent century in history. It's true. Hannah Arendt called it that. Two world wars, two totalitarian ideologies, civil wars, religious wars, ethnic wars . . . it doesn't end. It began at Sarajevo and ended with Kosovo. So what is happening to us so that we don't know how to live in peace with one another? What is happening to us so that we don't remember that one bullet in Sarajevo provoked a world war?

**Do we remember less well, do you think? Do you think one must look back and say, "We have learned our lessons so poorly that we are stepping backwards"?**

If we forget, we step backwards, because we go back to the abyss of ignorance. The nineteenth century was dominated by Napoleon. What was Napoleon's goal? Conquest. What was the twentieth century's? Conquest. One of the words that dominated our vocabulary was "conquest." Stalin wanted to conquer Eastern Europe and did. Hitler wanted to conquer the whole world and almost did. And now, after the two world wars, we want to conquer space. It's always "conquer." The money-makers conquer money in the markets. Other people conquer minds. The fanatics today are after our souls. So what does it mean, really? It means that certain words survive from one century into the other. And we are not wise enough or strong enough, perhaps not generous enough, to know that certain words are dangerous. They are carriers of death. And these words should be unmasked first and disarmed later.

In general, we use the wrong words. We've lost the ability to find the meaning of words. When there's a separation between word and meaning, then the words are in exile. And we are in exile. We exile ourselves by doing things we don't understand.

**Please help me understand that.**

I'll give you an example. A tragedy occurs somewhere in the world and we must, as human beings, take a human position to help its victims. But we don't know how to help the victims without beginning another war. Take Kosovo, for instance. We wanted to help the victims, the ethnic Albanians. And in the process a war went on. In the beginning there were only a hundred thousand victims, then over a million—a million people expelled from their homes, from their lives, from their identities. We didn't want that. We wanted to help them. But we don't know what to do. Yet power is here at our disposal. All we have to do is stretch out our hand.

**Isn't that an indication that we only really want to do things if they come easily? That our own moral purpose is far different from those moral purposes that have motivated us in the past?**

We have spoken so often, you and I, and we decided together that without its ethical component, history must go astray, because the carriers of history would do immoral things. In the thirties, Hitler's whole program was there to be seen. He said it openly in his book and in his speeches. He said he was going to do this and that. And yet the whole world was silent. If France had intervened in 1936 or 1938, and Britain, too, in 1939, there would have been no Second World War. Which means we must take a moral position and act on it. It's not easy. And we shouldn't look for easy solutions.

**You would never be one to withdraw and simply say, "I see what the moral solution must be, but the human race will not, and therefore let us all withdraw." Do you ever even entertain that notion?**

I'm not that naive. I know that you hear the words I use, because you are my friend. And I'm yours. But those who have power don't hear. It doesn't matter, we go on. We must go on. We knock on the door, sometimes, with our head. And one of the two will break, either the head or the door. One must do it. If not, what is the sense of our being in the world? What are we doing with our memories of our suffering, of our triumphs, of our tribulations, of our challenges, of our defeats?

**We tried to follow the moral principles that you set forth in terms of Kosovo. In the process, we read every day about people we killed. How do you deal with the point that we became executioners in our well-intentioned activities?**

Poorly. Badly. I say to myself, "Thank God I am not a general." I would be a very poor soldier anyway. At the same time, what is the alternative? To be complacent? Resigned? And let Milosevic do what he had been doing before the bombing and during the bombing? That, I think, would be irresponsible, immoral, and maybe even criminal.

**Didn't you find increasing numbers of people nevertheless saying, "We must withdraw. We cannot participate in these atrocities"?**

I didn't really hear people telling me, "Let's not do it at all." On the contrary, people said, "Since we've decided we must intervene for moral reasons, let's send troops." When I would speak, let's say at a university, students there would say, "Look, we understand the moral obligation." That, of course, was the basis, the moral obligation. Then, once we said it is moral, and that the moral imperative was to intervene, they would say, "Go ahead."

Let's be honest and compare what Milosevic was doing and what we were doing. What we did was to try to stop Milosevic, and in doing so, terrible things happened. The bombing of civilians, of course, is painful. Nobody wants to kill civilians. On the other hand, Milosevic wanted to expel the civilians and torment them and torture them and humiliate them and move them to despair. So it's atrocities, yes, when we speak of Milosevic. But not when we respond the way we did. Again, I don't see what else we could do.

We should be more careful, naturally. If I had to give advice to the generals, I would say, "Please be more precise, more focused. Installations, yes, but not people." But what do I know about these things? People asked me to sign all kinds of petitions. What right do I have to do that? I have never seen a tank from the inside. I've never been in a bomber. I don't know how many planes are needed. It's for the generals to decide. And I hope that they know what they are doing.

**But on the larger question, you sign the petitions in a way, morally, intellectually.**

That we should intervene, yes. With a heavy heart, because I'm against violence. You know me. I don't find any beauty, any salvation, in violence. I'm against war. War is murder. It's mass murder, collective murder. God knows I've seen what war can do to people, the grotesque stupidity of war. And the fact that people kill one another is something that I find abhorrent. I don't glorify it. I'm against those who glorify war, who celebrate war—or war heroes, even.

However, there is a just war. For instance, the fight that the Allied nations had undertaken, the war against Hitler, was a just war. And yet, how many were killed in that war? Hundreds of thousands of brave Allied soldiers. We should always be grateful to them and their example and their parents and their friends. So naturally there's a "but."

But here, I think of the victims. I see the children, always the children. On television, I see they are looking for their parents, who have disappeared, because the militia came and took the father away. The mother's running after the husband. And the children are there. So I have the right, therefore, to say, "Look." You must think first of the victims, always, everywhere.

I am for the proposal, which I think was submitted and accepted by the United Nations, that in certain cases interference is permitted when human rights are violated. Otherwise, what right would I have had to fight for the rights of the dissidents or the Soviet Jewish refuseniks? Or the Soviet Jews who wanted to stay there but live Jewishly, culturally, religiously, when the Soviet Union still existed? What right do I have today to fight against the dictatorships and the regimes that suppress and oppress their citizens? I think we should intervene.

**If we prevail, what will prevail—the notion that we will do it again and again?**

What should prevail is the gesture that civilized people with conscience do not abandon the victims of injustice. As you know, nothing is worse for the victim than to feel abandoned. And it breaks my heart to think that they would feel abandoned. We have no right to abandon them. And that should be, I think, the lesson. Wherever a dictator tries to do the same thing, there will be enough people in the world who will assume and accept the sacrifices necessary.

**Can there be an answer?**

You and I are teachers because we try to favor the question over the answer. Maybe the people of this century will learn from the experiences of the last century how to ask questions. Questions bring people together. Answers divide them. Fanatics have no questions; they give you the answer before they hear your question. And people of this century, to save themselves from many of the trials that plagued the previous century, will learn that to ask the question is more important than the answers.

**You remain the most somber optimist I know. But you say we must find a future in which what you describe now will be of the past. You still are a man of faith.**

Camus said it: The choice is being a weeping optimist or a smiling pessimist. So we smile. It doesn't mean that there is no reason for weeping. But what can we offer our young people? Only sadness? I think if that were the answer, I would stop. I would go on writing, but I wouldn't publish. I think they deserve something else. When I write a novel, usually the beginning is somber. Until I find a way out, I don't give it to the publisher. I must find a ray of hope, somewhere, anywhere.

**And do you find a ray of hope for our discussion of this new century?**

Yes. I see the young people—your children and grandchildren and my son and his children. I think of them. On one hand, it is very sad. I say, "Look what could happen to them." The legacy of the twentieth century is a warning. But then I say to myself, "They're young, they inherit the legacy, and they in turn will do something with it." And so I smile.

# INTERLUDE

Have you found that your teachings about the Holocaust have moved children of darkness and made them children of light?

Absolutely. I write little about the Holocaust now because so many others do. But I can testify that when a child, or even a grown-up, enters the world of that kind of literature, then they are no longer the same. That I can tell you. Of course, a person who does not care about humanity and only cares about machines doesn't read this literature. And if he or she reads, it doesn't matter. But I have seen what it did to children, how it changed their lives. I have seen adults, how it changed their lives.

You know who else reads this kind of literature? Cancer patients. Strange. I get many letters from cancer patients, because they, too, feel they're doomed. They are in a universe from which there is no way out. And they find something in this approach, in this possibility of hope.

# SEVEN

# The Anatomy of Hate

When at Boston University you concluded the first of your seminars on "The Anatomy of Hate," you said, "I had the feeling that most participants were afraid of the subject. Somehow they are afraid of facing the word 'hate.' " What did you mean?

The subject evokes and elicits violence and debased emotions, and therefore it's easier for a scientist or a scholar to use other words, nicer words. I had that feeling in Boston, where some of the best minds in the United States and Europe had come to take part in the gathering. But they did not address the subject. It wasn't "hate"; it was "conflict resolution," which is important. But why do people hate one another, and what is it about a human being that he or she should be capable of such hatred, often for no reason? Take anti-Semitism. The anti-Semite in Australia has never seen me, has never heard of me, and yet he or she hates me simply because I am Jewish. I'm speaking to you about hate. Do we mean "them"? Do they mean "us"? What is it about hate that brings people together only to destroy each other? So people are afraid of that challenge—and it is a challenge.

**You say, "Do we mean 'them'? Do they mean 'us'?" But is hate something else? Something more amorphous, unfocused?**

Oh, I think it's human, first of all. I think every human being is almost by definition capable of hatred. But what I learned in Boston is that a child, until the age of three, is not. A child begins to hate at the age of three. In other words, the child has been taught how to hate.

Now, what is hatred? Of course, it is bigotry, it is fanaticism, it's envy, it's jealousy, it's rancor, bitterness, all the elements. You can use any vocabulary, and the vocabulary may be transposed and transfixed into a different one, simply by changing the minus to plus or the plus to minus, and then what is good becomes bad.

**I'm a little puzzled, because at first it sounds as though you're saying to hate is to be human—**

Oh, no. No, no. I mean every human being is capable of hatred, but to hate is actually to dehumanize oneself. It's like being sick. Every person can be sick, but he has to fight it.

**Of course, then, there are the words, as you restate them, of the old song, "You've got to be taught to hate." But everyone seems to be taught. Is that an unfair observation?**

I think you are too pessimistic. Not everybody's taught to hate. In many places in the world today there is much bigotry and much fanaticism, and people are contaminated, of course. But I would also say that in every place in the world under the sun we are trying to fight hate in different ways. Whenever good educators meet, they try to vanquish hate. Whenever the good journalist is writing a good piece, a good column, I think, or doing a good TV program, it is automatically becoming a weapon against hate.

When I came here for the first time as a journalist, I took a cross-country trip with friends of mine. I was very poor. They had a car, and they took me with them. When I came to the South, and I saw a poster saying "For Whites Only," I was ashamed of being white. And I think that shame remained in our collective psyche. Because we should have been ashamed. But you must also admit that something happened to this country and to these people—that in a generation, one big generation maybe, we have changed not only the law, but also our mentality. To be a racist today is something shameful. There are still too many racists today—there are plenty of racist groups in this country—but still, you take a human being anywhere in this country, you will see that normally that human being will be embarrassed if he or she is called racist.

And then I was in Israel in 1967, during the war. I felt I had to be there because in the three weeks preceding the war, maybe you remember, there was fear. We were all convinced that Israel would lose the war. And I will not forget the humane way in which the Israeli soldiers treated the enemies. They were crying. I was in the desert and I saw how Israeli soldiers gave their water to the Egyptians. There was no hate in those Israeli soldiers.

**You said that in Boston there was a focus on "conflict resolution." Why do you think people moved to that? You**

say, because they were afraid. Afraid of what they feel in
themselves?

Afraid to touch something that is ugly. Conflicts have
been glorified, heroes have emerged out of conflicts, but
who ever emerged out of hate? So people don't like the
word "hate." Conflict resolution is a beautiful concept
and it's, by the way, necessary. In the United States, scholars in various universities have managed to come up with
theories about how to handle conflicts. But hate is something else. It's irrational, and who wants to deal with
irrational problems, irrational urges? And yet it's all
linked, I think. Hate is at the basis, at the core, of many
events that occurred in this century and are still occurring in many places under the sun today.

More so in this past century than before?

Maybe not, but we know more about them. In ancient
times there *were* wars, always.

But that's not what you're talking about?

No, because it was different. I would even say something else. Today, we manage—that means our civilization, unfortunately—to dehumanize hatred, or to push
hatred to such a level of absolutes that terrible crimes are
committed without hatred. Example: During the Second
World War, the killers in the death camps and the Ein-
satzgruppen in the Ukraine didn't really hate their victims. They viewed them as subhumans, and a human only
hates another human being. We realized then it's possible to envisage a tragedy incommensurate in its implications and scope, and yet all this could be done without
hatred.

I'm puzzled. You say that in the camps you bore witness to

the fact that, as you saw it, there was not hate, but there was . . . what?

It was something else. But then, you know, that is my hesitation, when I come to that period. I don't like to use other ideas, or previous concepts. I think it was a new event, a unique event that cannot be repeated, that has not been emulated and will not be emulated ever again.

I know this means a great deal to you—the uniqueness, the one-time-only quality of the Holocaust. But you and I have seen so much going on in the world that other people refer to as "holocausts."

I don't accept it. It's a dilution. It's a very sensitive area, because God knows I would not want to appear as someone who is indifferent or insensitive to the suffering of those minorities who are being killed and persecuted in many lands and many continents. But to compare it to Auschwitz is wrong. There was only one. There should never be another one. And once we say there were many, that means there may be many again. I don't think there could be or there should be. Remember, the Jew was illegal in Germany. It was the law that every Jew, any Jew, not only could, but must, be killed. That didn't happen to any other people. And I'm glad it didn't, in a way. Because, why? Why should other people suffer the way we did? We tell the tale of our nightmare and of our darkness in order to prevent other people from entering that nightmare or being penetrated by that nightmare.

And therefore you don't want to use it as a metaphor?

It's not a metaphor; it shouldn't be a metaphor. It's a point of reference, yes. Everything should be referred to it, but not compared to it.

How can I explain it to you? Naturally those Nazis

were educated to be anti-Semites. Anti-Semitism meant hatred. It still does. It meant hatred, of course, for almost twenty centuries on a religious level; we shouldn't deny that. On a religious level, many Christians, Catholics and Protestants, actually grew up hating Jews because that was the religious law, as though God had wanted them to hate his people, and it prepared the way to Nazism, there's no doubt about that.

But then, when it came to the killing, to this day I don't understand how it was possible—how could a man or a woman participate in the killing of ten thousand people a day and not even feel it? Now, had there been hate, it would not have been as systematic. Hate means a pogrom, an explosion, but during the war it was scientific. It was a kind of industry. They had industries and all they produced was death. Had there been hate, the laboratories would have exploded. They didn't. They went on. It was a parallel universe. When people came there, the killers killed, the victims died, the sky was blue, and somewhere a man who was in charge of the bookkeeping wrote, "Today they killed 10,494." It went on and on. Had there been hate, it would not have been possible.

**Is there hate today in the terms that you would use to define hate? Where do you see it?**

Oh, I don't compare. Cambodia was close to it, but even there it was different, because they educated the children to kill their parents. They didn't kill another people; they killed themselves. But the way they killed each other, for a purpose . . . In Germany, what was the purpose of killing Jews? To "free," to "purify" Germany from its Jewish element? The vocabulary, again, is not of hatred there; it's about prophylaxis. You exterminate cockroaches to purify your kitchen, and that was what they wanted to achieve.

**Maybe hatred itself wasn't dealt with at Boston sufficiently because it is so hard to define or to identify. We're not doing all that good a job ourselves.**

Because we are going around it and we are trying to enter it. Neither I nor you are willing to deal with something ugly.

**You've spoken of "the seduction of inhumanity." What is it that is so seductive about hatred, about inhumanity?**

To be able to hate somebody gives the hater a very strong feeling that he is superior. He knows the truth and I don't. He looks at me and he hates me because I'm a Jew, or because I'm an intellectual, or because I'm white, or black, or because I am not this or that, and *he* passes judgment. He knows that I'm wrong; he knows what I shouldn't do. He knows the answers, I only know the questions. He needs to humiliate me in order to feel sure of himself. He needs to imprison me and only then does he feel free. It gives the hater tremendous power in his own eyes.

For a hater, there is also seduction. And there is seduction for those who serve the hater, let's say somebody who works for a dictator. There is the will to believe that somebody is a leader, somebody has the authority, somebody knows what to do. You remember why Mussolini was elected? Because he said the trains would run on time. And with that slogan he won the elections.

**Have you ever hated anyone? Or anything?**

I'm sure I had hatred in me when I was young and I was angry. But real hate, let's say after the war, I must say I had none. I was shielded. I could have had it, and maybe I should have.

**Why do you say that?**

Because it was a normal reaction, after all. After such an experience, it would be normal for us to hate the killers, hate the accomplices. Why not?

**I've never heard you say that before.**

It's true. I feel it would have been normal. I don't think it happened, but it could have happened, and the fact that it didn't happen is abnormal. I had to choose between two options of humanity. And I would rather choose this one.

**Do you regret for yourself that it did not happen?**

Of course not, of course not. I must tell you I'm grateful to history, to God, I don't know to whom, for having been spared. I survived; I don't know why. I swear to you. I was too young, I was too weak. But because I survived by chance, I had to give meaning to my survival. That's really what I believe in. Mind you, if I had felt that hate would lead me somewhere, would give me or humanity an answer, maybe I would have tried it. But I never felt hate.

**You would have been poorer had you hated.**

I think I would have destroyed myself. That is one of the lessons of hate. That hate destroys not only the hated, it destroys the hater. And I think it would have destroyed us. What happened after the war? What happened was that after the liberation I got sick. I was in a coma for ten days. And then almost immediately I went to France and I began studying again. I threw myself into the books that I had left closed, and I plunged into that universe of ideas, debates, and memories. That saved me. That meant I wanted to open up again. I became extremely religious, extremely pious. I went through a religious experience as profound as I had in 1943, just before I went into that camp. That saved me, the passion for study.

**You haven't stated it, but there seems to be a conflict—**

Oh, there is a conflict. I remember in 1945 when the war ended for me—April 11. The Americans came into Buchenwald. I was terribly weak and sick—alone, desperate, numb. We hadn't eaten for so many days. And since April 5 we were close to death, literally, because the Germans were trying to evacuate the camp. They would take out ten thousand people a day and ship them off to the unknown. And for some reason, I don't know why, we in the children's block remained behind. Then the Americans came in. I'll never forget these Americans. At one point there were some black soldiers, the first black soldiers I had ever seen. And they were crying. *They* were crying with anger. They were angry at the killers much more than we were. And they were throwing us whatever they had—you know, K rations and bread and chocolate. What we wanted to do first, though, before eating, was to have a religious service. And we had a religious service. So instead of going and committing acts of anger and wrath and bloodshed, we prayed to a God who had abandoned us.

**There are those who say that religion is itself, if not a provocateur, a key to hate in some ways.**

Could be. Look at Khomeini, and what Iran was doing. How many wars are fought on behalf of God? And how much hatred has been spread in the name of love for God? Of course, all this is possible. It happened. In our religion, take the Bible. The Bible, I believe, is one of the most humanizing documents that exist in recorded history, and yet there are tough pages. Like what are we supposed to do to our enemies? When Joshua came into the Holy Land—the conquest of Canaan wasn't something that I look at with pride, not at all.

**At your Boston conference, Conor Cruise O'Brien said, "The cult of the nation proved to be the most efficient engine for the mobilization of hatred and destruction that the world has ever known." I made my own note, a question, a word: "Religion." Hasn't religion been an even more efficient engine?**

Why compare? The moment you compare, it's wrong. There has been enough hatred propagated because of nationalism and enough hatred because of religion. Both are bad. In other words, the moment a religion says, "I alone possess truth," it may become a vehicle of hate, because anyone who says, "No, I am the one," is hated. The same is true of nationalism. The moment I say that my nation is more important than yours, worthier than yours, it becomes a reason for hate.

**In the one instance, though, we turn then to a kind of internationalism—to a United Nations or some parallel organization. Do you feel the same way about religion?**

I don't even think it's possible in the political arena. I don't think that nations will give up their sovereignty. Not in our lifetime. I don't think that we will ever have a world government. I wish we could, but we won't.

**Do you mean "ever," or "in our lifetime"?**

No nation is giving up sovereignty in our lifetime to have a world government. It will always face opposition; and you will have other people who will say, No, we want to be alone. That's why I am not really that utopian. I think we should simply try to educate, to be more tolerant. That's a minimum. Meaning that I, as a Jew, really believe that the Jewish tradition contains beauty and morality for me, as a Jew, and I also believe that the Christian has exactly the same right to say that Christianity makes beauty and morality for him or her. If the Christian will not try to convert me, I would respect the Christian very much.

**So you are not looking for unity, you are looking for diversity?**

Diversity and respect, yes.

**And do you think we will find that respectful diversity?**

I would begin in a very small way, person to person, teacher and student, student and student. It's enough. I think I told you once that when I was young I was convinced that I could hasten the coming of the Messiah. Every Jewish child believes that. If I could only pray enough, with enough fervor and enough purity, I could hasten universal redemption. Now I know I will never do that. What I think we should do now, what I think I can do now, is bring redemption for one minute to one person. And I believe it's really simplistic that whenever two persons reach an understanding based on a kind of mutual respect for dignity and with a smile, redemption has been hastened. So while it is limited in scope, it appeals to me.

**Then I turn to your conferences on hate and I wonder what you try to achieve with them. What is your objective?**

It may surprise you: not much. All I really want is to bring people together. I have a firm conviction that if we bring people around the same table, something will happen, something good. So that, for me, is the first aim and the first goal. Anything afterward is an unexpected reward. The first reward is to bring people together, speaking different languages, coming from different disciplines, representing different areas of concern and loyalty, and yet all of us trying, around the table, at the same time, after all, to help solve a little bit of the problem that is plaguing us, has been plaguing us for so many centuries.

**That isn't the way scholars function, is it?**

No. There is a marvelous sentence in the Talmud. The Talmud says that scholars increase peace in the world, so my teacher Saul Lieberman used to say that proved the Talmud had a sense of humor. Because to say that scholars bring peace into the world . . . anyone who knows the academic community knows how to quarrel.

But I believe that if you manage to gather people and you motivate them enough, simply to be there and listen and talk and open up and not to care about glory or beginning an argument or making a point, it is a miracle. I think it's beautiful. Who knows? Then a statement may be formulated, a manifesto may be composed. Can you imagine if we have another session of "The Anatomy of Hate" and we emerge with a manifesto against hate, signed by great scholars and statesmen and poets and writers? Why not?

**What would you say?**

I would try to show the danger of hate because hate corrupts. It corrupts the values, it corrupts the sight, and hate actually is a destroyer. It's not death yet, but it destroys, and therefore hate is always at the service of death, and I would try to show, with examples, from so many places, how hate has destroyed the victim and the environment, because all around the hater and the hated there are millions of people who must choose to become either their accomplices or their fellow victims.

**Is that a notion that is understood? That hate destroys the hater?**

Well, it has to be made clear. That's what I feel. If the hater were to know how much his or her hate will destroy him or her, I think that would be the first opening in the wall. That means the hater will hesitate a second before continuing to hate. Now, we are not going to change the Ku Klux Klan or the white supremacists, who are fanatics about it. I don't even work on them. But there are other people who are prey to fanaticism. There is, to them, I imagine, a certain glory in saying, "Only what is I is good. Our group is the best, and we should help our people, our community alone." There is the danger there. If we would strive to explain the danger of hate to the hater, maybe because of self-preservation we could achieve something.

# INTERLUDE

It almost seemed that after the Bitburg incident, when President Reagan visited a German cemetery where SS soldiers were buried, there were more people willing to express anti-Semitism openly, with no secrets—even to make threats upon you. How do you explain that?

They were feeling suppressed hate, and whenever a public event occurs which involves the highest office in the land, it is like a catalyst. It removes the obstacle. It removes the mask. And people speak the way they want to speak. And therefore, the anti-Semite became more anti-Semitic.

At the same time, the good person became better. That is not new. You know, it was so even during the war. What I had seen during the war taught me an important lesson: Tragedies do not change people. They simply deepen the being in them. The good did not become bad. The bad did not become good. What happened was that the good became better—and the bad became worse.

# EIGHT

# Capital Punishment: An Eye for an Eye?

**How must we look at capital punishment in terms of our moral responsibilities? How can we measure it in moral terms?**

Well, traditionally, capital punishment is here either to punish someone who has committed a capital crime or to deter other people from doing the same thing. Personally, I am against capital punishment.

**Why?**

For many reasons. I do not believe a civilized society should be at the service of death. I don't think it's human to become an agent of the Angel of Death. Death is always a blemish on creation, according to the tradition that I come from. Death is a scandal, and the fact that people die should not help us make more people die. Whatever we do, we must affirm life. Not only the beauty or the justice or the truth inherent in life, but life. Simply living is an extraordinary adventure that happens only once to the person in us, or the person that we are. Whenever death strikes, it should move people to close their eyes and think about life, about the living, about the responsibility of man and woman for the living. And therefore I don't like to think that we are here to kill even a killer.

**When you say you "don't like to think," there seems to me to be lurking behind that—**

The "but," right?

**—the "but," the compunction.**

First of all, let's see why I'm against capital punishment, and maybe we'll see if there are hesitations or a certain recalcitrance.

In capital punishment, there's a certain element of staging. It becomes a spectacle, and I'm against staging death. In France during the revolution, there were crowds who would gather in the morning, waiting. And the women would knit, the people would talk, and they would do whatever they wanted to while watching an amusing, entertaining spectacle of a person being put to death. Today, although it's a new era even in that field, until thirty or forty years ago people could watch the execution of a man. Now it is witnessed by journalists, judges, the prosecutor, the warden, and the priest. It is a ritual. That is not something that I would approve of.

**I believe it was a public television station that asked for the right to televise an execution, mostly on the grounds that if it were televised, the horror that you and others feel for**

capital punishment today would become the basis for an effective resistance to the whole nasty business.

That is possible. But at the same time, it could inspire a candidate for committing murder to do precisely that. Because there's a strange distortion in the psyche of a murderer. The murderer usually wants to be front-line. He wants to be on stage. A murderer wants to be someone who has done something that has not been done before to that person. We are born once, we die once. So he's doing it. And therefore, when you give him this opportunity to appear at center stage, there he is, or she is, at the very center. And at the center he or she remains until the last minute. And maybe, in his distorted mind, it would be appealing.

**You talked about society taking life as a denial of the affirmation that you want to make of life itself. But aren't we, in terms of capital punishment, at the same time affirming the value of life by taking the life of the person who took other lives?**

Here comes the "but." There are certain cases where I'm very close to saying, "Well, there must be exceptions." I'll give you the example of Israel. In Israel, there is no capital punishment except for those Nazis who have committed crimes against humanity or against the Jewish people. The only person who was executed in Israel was Adolf Eichmann. The only one. During the Eichmann trial, I went there to cover it. Eichmann was sentenced to death. Afterward, a great Jewish philosopher began obtaining signatures for petitions to have Eichmann spared. I didn't sign that petition. That's the exception.

**Tell me, though, why you did not.**

I felt that Eichmann, a man who helped exterminate, kill, massacre so many thousands of lives, should not be spared. If the court had decided not to execute him, I would have also been in favor, but once the court decided to sentence him to death, reluctantly I felt that was an exception.

**Do you wish that you could go back and eliminate the spectacle? It was a spectacle, his trial, as was his death.**

The death was not, the trial was. But spectacle in the best sense of the word. I have seen trials that became educational vehicles of extraordinary importance—the Barbie trial in France, Eichmann in Israel. I heard—because I wasn't there—that Eichmann's death was totally discreet. Forgive me for the word. But nobody was there except those who had to be.

**You talk about the tens of thousands who died because of this man. Now, there's a calculus. What is the number that must be reached before you will accept capital punishment?**

It's not a matter of numbers.

**What is it, then?**

The event itself. When a man is involved in the Final Solution, meaning in sentencing an entire people to death, I think the measure is different. Those who were killed at Nuremberg, who were executed the same way as Eichmann—I wasn't for capital punishment then, but I approve the capital punishment meted out to them. They were involved in something that was beyond the pale, beyond the human mind, beyond history. They had done something that had never been done before, period.

They had sentenced a people to die. Not only those who were in their country, but any Jew, anywhere. You in America were sentenced to death. And your children who weren't born yet were sentenced to death. Therefore it's a special category. We must learn from that special category, and I learned from it. I learned that death is always a scandal and I am against that anywhere. But I accept this kind of judgment of justice.

**Let me ask you: Is there some way of defining the exceptions you would make?**

To me, the murder of children would surely deserve to be an exception.

**Why?**

Because children represent innocence, helplessness. We bring children into this world because we want those children to take over, to become the custodians of our fears, our hopes. They should shape tomorrow's world, which must, thanks to them, be a better one. And here comes their wanton murderer, with one bullet, or bomb, simply because these children were there. I think that something must be done. Maybe there is another answer. But something harsh must be envisaged to discourage these criminals and punish them—something that is as harsh as death but is not death. Maybe.

**Certainly there are people whose involvement with the victims of a murderer would lead them to say, "This is an exception." But if we make these exceptions, where do we stop?**

Your question is a good question. Suppose there is a serial killer. For the victim's family, this serial killer is as atrocious as Eichmann must have been for us. Who am I to judge whose pain is sharper and whose is not? I have no right to downgrade anyone else's pain.

**My objective, obviously, is not to say, "Elie Wiesel, you made a mistake" or anything of the kind, but rather to see what sympathy or empathy you have for those who ask for capital punishment.**

Oh, I hear, of course, the arguments, I see the arguments, I read them, and I understand them also, but I am against capital punishment. The arguments would have you believe that the only way to prevent murder is to kill the murderer or to threaten the murderer with death. It may work, but I don't think so.

**You're saying you think there is no deterrent.**

A person who is really a killer is so taken by death that that person is no longer afraid of death. By giving death, that person has accepted his own death. Other people may say I'm wrong, and I'm sure they have good arguments, but I have seen too much death.

**And your sympathy for those who need, somehow or other, to have vengeance?**

Oh, vengeance is never a real response.

**But why?**

It reduces the tragedy. Vengeance is an impulsive act. It lasts a minute. And then what? Suppose a son's father is killed by a murderer. Okay. That son goes and kills the murderer, so you obtain—what? The tragedy is not as true as it was before. There is something else now in the equation. We cannot start taking vengeance because then we wouldn't stop. If my contemporaries had wanted to become avengers, we would have set Europe on fire, and there would have been no one to condemn us. Can you imagine these thousands of young Jews who had just come out of the forests as partisans, or as inmates of the death camps? Weapons were all around us. We could have gone anywhere and killed. But we didn't do that.

After the war, the Germans were afraid. They weren't afraid of the Americans. Nor were they afraid of the French. Of the Russians, yes. But above all, they were afraid of the Jews. Somehow they felt that the Jews would come back and avenge the blood that was shed. And it didn't happen. There were no acts of vengeance.

**Elie, was that not done at all?**

I think it was done by some Russian war prisoners. And really, I don't condemn them. I understand that the day the camp was liberated, they seized American jeeps, took weapons, went to Weimar, and became avengers. I think that among those Jewish inmates who survived their ordeal, there weren't many—I don't even know one—who did the same. I imagine there may have been a few. But we really didn't do that.

**Because of your religion, your training?**

I was too young to be thinking in those terms. It's something else. Self-preservation, perhaps. Where do you stop? You know where to begin—the SS first, right? But then there were support groups who helped the SS. And then the bystanders. And then you go back to Hungary— there were quite a few Hungarian fascists who helped the SS in my own town. They hurt and beat up more Jews than the Germans did. The same is true of Romania and Poland and the Ukraine. Where do you stop? It would be a bloodbath.

**So that you find at the basis of one's personal morality a sense of survival?**

I think that it worked out that way and I don't think it was a conscious decision. It has something to do with . . . in Hebrew, you call it *zechut avot*—the merit of our fathers, ancestral merit. There was someone in my subconscious who helped me, who saved me. My grandfather, or my great-grandfather, said, "Don't do that. It's not for you. We have never done that." Jewish history for two thousand years was a history of hatred and persecution, and imagine if we had taken vengeance each time. Memory is the best vengeance. What the killer is really afraid of is the memory of a person that he or she has killed.

**Your frequent statement that you must deal with everything in terms of its moral consequences—where does that sense come from?**

It comes from learning, from absorbing, from remembering. My memory did not begin with me. My memory began before me, and if my memory absorbs all the other memories, it becomes a kind of collective repository. When I grow up, I commit not only my own name, and my own honor and my own life, but the name and the honor of my predecessors. If I do something wrong, then my grandfather, somehow, and his name are at stake. Moses' honor is at stake. When you think in those terms, then you are careful.

**But we can't assume there is unanimity about capital punishment or about any of the moral issues before us. Whose moral terms are right and whose are wrong?**

Sure, I wouldn't say that those who are for capital punishment are immoral, absolutely not. I understand them. They have their own argument and their own reasons and their own humanity. When they say, "We want to prevent further murder," they have an argument. It's a very personal attitude.

**Are you asking only that we be sure to think and feel in those terms, whatever they may be for us?**

I would like whatever I do with certainty to have a small spark of uncertainty: "Maybe I'm wrong." And I think that is the same for morality: "I am not so sure." And I can push it very far then, of course. What about the murderer? Am I sure the murderer, then, is always wrong? If I say I have to be uncertain, maybe the murderer is right. No? There are limits, of course. And what is Judaism? A set of limits. That's how it began—you don't go beyond the limit. In the beginning, it was monotheism or "Thou shalt not kill." I'm too Jewish not to accept limits.

**Too Jewish not to be involved in those ambiguities?**

I accept the ambiguity because tolerance in Jewish doctrines is inspiring. The Talmud, which is one of the great masterworks of all time, is full of ambiguity and full of dialogue. It is the only body of work in recorded history where the minority's views have been preserved. It's nothing but dialogue. An example of tolerance and understanding.

**I've always known you to be a person deeply sympathetic to the needs of others. The need to wreak revenge, to find some outlet for the angers and the damage that's been done . . . you must be sympathetic to that need.**

I understand that. The Oklahoma bombing, for instance, is a nightmare. When I saw these children in Oklahoma, I was seized with rage.

**It's hard for me to see you seized with rage.**

Quiet rage, silent rage. I saw the faces of the children. I

saw one marvelous policeman who thought he saved a
baby. And he said, "It's my baby." It wasn't his, but it
became his. It was dead.

I understand those people who want capital punishment for certain capital crimes. After a trial, the parents
or the children of the victim say, "We demand justice,"
meaning the death penalty. But I cannot tell you that I
would like to see me, myself, giving you a kind of judgment, that this is how it should be. Maybe we don't have
enough imagination. Let me think about it. I still believe,
you know, in encounters. I believe in people meeting simply to try to explore an issue and see where it leads. I
would like, for instance, if the law professors and law
deans and scholars and judges could have a kind of
conference and see if there is anything that is as harsh
as death but is not death. Maybe we should—I don't
know—build something on an island and there should
be mandatory life imprisonment with harsh conditions.
But life for life . . . The Bible says yes.

**Yes indeed.**

In the Bible we have so many laws that impose capital
punishment, but the laws are never to be implemented.

**What do you mean?**

If you read the Bible, you get the feeling you can't do
anything. If you violate the Sabbath, capital punishment. If a child is not respectful toward the parents,
capital punishment. If a whole city becomes sinful, the
whole city suffers capital punishment. But—here comes
the "but"—the laws are there, yet we must do everything
possible to go around them. There are harsh laws in the
Bible for homosexuality—capital punishment. And yet

it was never implemented. The Bible says that anyone who comes to kill you, you better kill him first. How do you know until it is too late?

All this, I believe, really tells us to wait and ponder. Maybe the conclusion will be, at a certain point in time, that you must use capital punishment because there is no other choice—but that you should wait a bit. If I told you, in the Talmud, about the extraordinary distance our sages have gone to avoid implementation of a death penalty . . . The Talmudic interpretation of these laws is so human. For instance, in ancient times no person could be indicted and condemned unless there were two witnesses watching the person doing what the person did. Even then, the person had to be warned before committing the act.

**You mean, "We are watching."**

Watching. If the person was not warned, the case was thrown out of court. Or if there were not two witnesses. Murder means not to follow a warning, and to do it in front of witnesses. Even then, the two witnesses were interrogated and cross-examined to the degree of torture. In a way, the judges were hoping they would contradict themselves or maybe there would be a draw. Even then, if they told the truth, they were told, "Now, you should know you are the first to throw the stones. So don't think you can simply say what you are saying and get away and get home and drink water and eat bread. Your words commit you." There are so many laws about it. Every capital case was brought before a tribunal. The tribunal was composed of twenty-three judges. Now, if the verdict was guilty, it was unanimously thrown out of court.

**Explain that, please.**

Because it was inconceivable, first of all, to find twenty-three Jews who will feel unanimous on anything. But the main reason is that we couldn't believe that among the twenty-three judges who were trying one person alone—at that time they didn't have defense lawyers—not one should feel sorry for that man and come up with some defense. Here comes the amazing question: Suppose one judge was convinced that this defendant is innocent. Now, if he says "Innocent," then he will die. In order to save the defendant, he must vote with the others to make it unanimous. So, what should the judge do? You see the complication, the complexity of the issue of capital punishment in Talmudic law and biblical law?

Let's say both of us are here in this studio, and there's only one door to another room. In that room, which has no windows, somebody's there—a secretary, preparing your script or your questions or your answers or your research. Suddenly a man arrives, her lover, with a knife, saying, "Where is she?," and he runs inside, and you and I hear her screaming. He comes out with blood on his knife. What do you say? Guilty? No, because we have not witnessed the crime. But wait—blood . . . circumstantial evidence? Two thousand years ago, self-incriminating evidence was thrown out of court and this man could go free because there were no witnesses.

**But Elie, one could tell this story with the sense of the glory of that tradition, or one could tell it with the sense of how nonsensical it is to let someone who committed murder go free.**

But you know the old rule: better a hundred murderers go free than one innocent die.

Then you've just finished describing what happens in the Bible itself. The words are there, the acts do not follow.

Right.

You think that is the Bible's recognition of the need to be sympathetic toward those of us who feel such anger at those who have murdered?

I think on the surface it's a simple act of God saying, "I give life, and you have no right to remove it. I am the owner of life, all life. Mine, yours, anyone's." Which means the victim's and the killer's. So God says, "All right. You have taken life, I'll take yours."

That isn't what "an eye for an eye" means.

Oh, no. "An eye for an eye" is not that. "An eye for an eye," really, in the Bible, was misinterpreted. That means the *value* of—an eye for an eye. If somebody took out my eye, I'm not going to take out his. It simply means that he has to pay damages for what I have lost in losing my eyesight.

Don't you think those who argue for the deterrent effect of capital punishment are saying there is too much of that—equating the taking of a life with ten to twenty years in jail?

Again, I really cannot answer you on that. I understand the pain of the father whose child has been killed. I understand the pain of people who have become orphaned. But to come out and say, "I am therefore for capital punishment," I cannot hear myself say that.

I'm aware that one thing you don't say in opposition to capital punishment is, "Perhaps a mistake has been made. Perhaps we have identified the wrong persons responsible for this act."

I know there have been cases of mistaken identity, but still . . .

**You know I don't agree with you.**

What mainly preoccupies me is institutionalizing death. I cannot see myself accepting it.

## INTERLUDE

You are enormously aware of the past because of your profound involvement with the great Hebrew prophets. Does that give you any sense of change in what we are like as human beings?

Oh, if Jeremiah were to come back today, he would say exactly the same thing. And once more, I think, he would not be heard. The prophets were the most tragic of all people because when they spoke, nobody listened. They were punished for speaking, and God allowed them to be punished for speaking. I think not a single prophet except Moses died a natural death. They were all punished—Isaiah, Jeremiah, Amos, all of them. I love them because they are so clumsy. They have to speak, they're forced to speak. God makes them speak, God gives them the words. And yet at the end he allows them to suffer and die—for speaking, for doing his will. So I have profound sympathy for them and I occasionally teach them to my students. To me, the prophet is a striking symbol. The Jewish tradition is illustrated by its prophets, really. Others had oracles and idols. We had prophets.

**What's the difference?**

The prophet is mortal. The prophet always takes the side of the weak, of the poor. The prophet was never elected. He was not even appointed except by God, which means by a voice that came to him or a vision that he had at night. The prophet always speaks truth to power. The prophet would come to the king and say, "You shall not do that or you'll be punished." And he told the king things that a king didn't want to hear. In any other civilization, the prophet would be executed right away. Not there, because the prophet had a status.

Now, what is the prophet's role? To defend those who are defenseless—the sick, the underprivileged, as we call them today. Those who need defense from anyone—even from God. The prophet at times had to take the side of the people. But if he didn't, he was punished. They all suffered. Why? Because they were too harsh with their people. That isn't fair. God told them to be harsh. And they were harsh. And therefore they were punished.

**Sounds like a discussion we once had about Job.**

Exactly. Now, I am on the side of Job, always. And I am on the side of the victim, always. And sometimes we are victims of God.

# NINE

# Taking Life: Can It Be an Act of Compassion and Mercy?

**"Mercy killing"—that's a phrase that's frequently used. Could you embrace such a concept?**

Impulsively, instinctively, I would be against it. "Mercy killing" is a frightening expression. These two words are incompatible. Killing is against mercy; mercy is against killing. And yet I know that the problem is a problem. There are certain cases when a person suffers so much as to want to die. Do we have the right to force him or her to go on living and suffering?

**No more, I would suspect, than we have the right to prevent him or her from going on living and perhaps suffering.**

Well, that's again a question. In some nations, suicide is forbidden. If the attempt fails and the person survives, he or she goes to jail.

**But may society interfere with an individual's choice?**

I suppose that if I witnessed the last moments of a person who wants to commit suicide, I would first try to persuade that person that death is never the answer.

**But what is your sense of the concept of society interfering with an individual's choice?**

It so happens that at Boston University, where I have been teaching for so many years, I have been giving a course about suicide in literature—in the Bible, in antiquity, in modern literature—either about the writer or the character in a book who commits suicide. And I learned quite a lot, really. In the Bible, for instance, very few commit suicide. King Saul did, and he got away with it. Suicide is forbidden in Jewish law, and yet we celebrate King Saul.

**How?**

He is a king, and we feel sorry for him. We don't condemn him for falling on his sword.

**Then how do you rationalize the injunction against suicide?**

There's a beautiful story: Two masters in the Talmud speak about two persons walking in the desert who have only one jug of water—enough for one to survive. What should they do? One man says, "Let them divide the water. Friends will remain friends. Even if it means that they die." But the other says, "No. The owner of the water should drink the water." Why? The reason is, my life is not my own. The owner of my life, in the Jewish tradition—and I think in any religious tradition—is God. So I have no right to do with my life what I want.

**I was recently reading *Night*, that first wonderful autobiographical publication of yours. You talk about the tale of the two men in the desert—that it is not mine to choose that I should share my life. I was thinking of what you had**

written in *Night* of your father's death and the question that came up: He was dying. There was very limited food and drink. Should you try to share yours with him or shouldn't you, since he really couldn't take that food, your food? What was the nature of the moral resolution?

Oh, the moral resolution was to stay with my father, naturally. And I stayed. It was a thought that for a moment passed through me because somebody else told me that. He said, "Don't think of your father. Anyway, it's too late, and you must think of yourself." But I had learned even then, without knowing it, that those who gave me such advice were wrong. The Germans wanted us to behave that way. They wanted us to be selfish, self-centered, ignoring and forgetting everything about all others to survive. It was a world of ice. Only those who were connected with another person through an ideal or through family had a chance to survive.

But how does that relate to the injunction that it was not your life to share?

First of all, honor your father. But it was even more than that. I became so close to my father then that I felt I would not survive him. In fact, I didn't. Afterward, I wasn't really alive. I would have given my bread, everything I had, for him.

And done violence to a Talmudic injunction?

Oh, absolutely.

Tell me about that. You say, "Absolutely."

First of all, at that point one doesn't think in those terms. One acts intuitively, impulsively. One acts as a human being, as a son. My father was the only person in my family who remained with me. And I loved him there more than ever before. So I would have lost my own humanity, my own self-respect, my own desire to live, had I acted differently. Those conditions are beyond our understanding.

Now, suppose I had thought, "Now, what should I do?" There were cases, I know, when certain people went to a rabbi in the camp to ask for a judgment. I didn't. If I had thought about the Talmud even then, I would have found enough reasons to justify my behavior. Because in the Talmud, the law that I just quoted to you is about two friends, but not about a father and a son. Father and son, whatever they own, they own together. So the jug of water would be their common property. I could have found the truth, but I didn't think in those terms. I really wanted to be with my father and live for him.

**And if you were the rabbi who was asked this question?**

Same thing. I would have also said, "First of all, *'Kabed et avichah v'et eemchah'*—'Honor thy father and mother.' "

**Above all else.**

Above all else. Because it's from the Ten Command-ments. But then the next sentence, *"L'maan ya-arichun yamchah"*—"So that you shall live long"—could be such an irony, because the second part surely was in con-tradiction to the first: By honoring my father, I would likely have died.

**What should we understand then about the nature, the function, the purpose, of Talmudic injunctions, biblical injunctions, spiritual injunctions?**

Well, they are there to help you. Very often in your life you are alone. And in those times, I was alone. Whatever I knew was of small consequence. The only thing that mattered to me was that weak, defeated human being who was my father. I rarely speak about that, you know. I have written about it. I rarely speak about those times.

**Too painful?**

It's painful. Also, I don't like to reveal myself that much. And also because I always had a feeling that people wouldn't understand. You do, because you and I have become very close friends. You know, even if I don't say it, you know what I said.

**What do you mean, "People wouldn't understand"?**

They would be incapable. The stories that I want to tell, that I feel I must tell, I most often keep to myself. Because I feel nobody would comprehend. I know people read and explain. Some people are moved. But I do know that no one will know what I know. No one will know what we who were there know. That knowledge cannot be communicated. And it pains me, it haunts me, because this is exactly what the killers wanted to attain. They pushed their brutality, their cruelty, beyond the limits of language, so that when we tell the tale, nobody knows what we are talking about. And yet—my favorite words—

**And yet—**

—we try. Maybe five hundred years from now, someone will sit here or anywhere and pick up a book that you or I have written and that person will feel more than the person today does.

**It certainly will be true of *Night*. In fact, I was going to ask if you would read these last pages. In a sense, I began there.**

[*Reading:*] "I knew that my father must not drink. But he pleaded with me so long that I gave in. Water was the worst poison that he could have. But what else could I do for him? With water, without water, it would all be over soon. And then he said, 'You, at least, have some mercy on me.' Have mercy on him. I, his only son. A week went by like this. 'This is your father, isn't it?' asked the head of the block. 'Yes.' 'He is very ill.' I answered, 'The doctor won't do anything for him.' And he said, 'The doctor can't do anything for him now. Neither can you.' He put his great, hairy hand on my shoulder and added, 'Listen to me, boy. Don't forget that you are in a concentration camp. Here every man has to fight for himself. He cannot think of anyone else, even of his father. Here there are no fathers, no brothers, no friends. Everyone lives and dies for himself alone. I'll give you a sound piece of advice. Don't give your ration of bread and soup to your old father. There is nothing you can do for him. And you are killing yourself. Instead you ought to have his ration.'

"I listened to him without interrupting. He was right, I thought in the most secret region of my heart, but I dared not admit it. 'It's too late to save your old father,' I said to myself. 'You ought to be having two rations of bread, two rations of soup.' Only a fraction of a second, but I felt guilty. I ran to find a little soup to give my father. But he did not want it. All he wanted was water. 'Don't drink water,' I said. 'Have some soup.' 'I'm burning,' said he. 'Why are you so unkind to me? Some water.' I brought him some water. Then I left the block for a roll call. But I turned around and came back again. I lay down on the top bunk. Invalids were allowed to stay in the block, so I would be an invalid myself. I would not leave my father.

"There was silence all around now. In front of the block the SS were giving orders. An officer passed by the beds. My father begged me, 'My son, some water. I'm burning. My stomach.' 'Quiet over there!' yelled the officer. 'Eliezer,' went on my father, 'some water.' The officer came up to him and shouted at him to be quiet. But my father did not hear him. He went on calling me, calling me. The officer dealt him a violent blow on the head with his truncheon. I did not move. I was afraid. My body was afraid of also receiving a blow. Then my father made a rattling noise, and it was my name, 'Eliezer.' I could see that he was still breathing, spasmodically. I didn't move.

"When I got down after roll call I could see his lips trembling as he murmured something. Bending over him, I stayed gazing at him for over an hour, engraving into my soul the picture of his bloodstained face, his shattered skull. Then we had to go to bed. When I climbed into my bunk above my father, he was still alive. It was January 28, 1945.

"I awoke on January 29 at dawn. In my father's place lay another invalid. They must have taken him away before dawn and carried him to the crematory. He must still have been breathing. There were no prayers at his grave. No candles were lit to his memory. His last word was my name. A summons, to which I did not respond. I did not weep. But it pained me that I could not weep. But I had no more tears. And in the depths of my being, in the recesses of my weakened conscience, I might perhaps have found something like, 'Free at last.' "

**What do we do with people who assist others, out of mercy and compassion, to end their lives? Not lives taken in Auschwitz, but lives of the terminally ill?**

I don't think I can give you a general answer. I believe every human being is a universe in himself. I think every human being represents humanity as such. And therefore I will say that every case should be examined and explored as a special and unique case. Which means all the arguments for and against have to be advanced again as if the case were the first and the last.

I just got some letters . . . there is a group that supports physician-assisted suicide. They are ready to give Dr. Kevorkian a kind of medal or something. Some of my students, one of whom did a doctorate on suicide, are outraged that he should be honored. They want me to protest. My problem is that I am not in the field. I don't think I should get involved. But I also don't think a law, simply a law, should make things that easy—to say, "Therefore we have the right to end one's life because the law allows it." In every case there should be much soul-searching and it should involve an effort, a spiritual effort, a moral effort.

I'm always shivering when I read statistics that so many American teenagers are committing suicide. And more, of course, are contemplating suicide. That means they have given up on our society. In Israel, it's different, because it is a young state built on ancient soil. They have their own problems with suicide. Recently, I read the book *Suicides in the Army,* about recruits who cannot take it for some reasons. Probably good reasons. To the person who committed suicide, I must grant that it was for a good reason.

**Why must you grant that?**

I'm against suicide, of course. But once the person has committed suicide, I cannot treat that person with disrespect.

**The choice?**

The choice. And the ultimate gesture. It is the ultimate protest.

**Generally, though, you maintain a very different approach to life. You celebrate it.**

Well, how can I oppose death if not by celebrating life? There is a beautiful saying in Talmudic literature, that in our weakness, we can celebrate a strength. One minute before I die, I am immortal. A minute of life is more important than all the books about life.

**A minute of what life? What kind of life? That is a question I believe you have asked at times.**

I will say any life. Whether that life is being spent correctly or not is not for me to decide. I am not God, nor his messenger.

**Are you speaking as a survivor when you say that about any moment of life?**

Oh, I speak as I. And I am a survivor. I'm a Jew. I'm an American. I'm a French writer. I'm a teacher. It's all together. The "I" is the sum total of the human being. I am the teacher because I was the student. And I'm trying to do something with our knowledge.

The real problem, after the war, when I was very young, was not that we didn't know, but that we knew too much. All of a sudden, at my age—I was sixteen or so—I knew so much. Too much. And unless we do something with such knowledge, we could be crushed by it. We had to adjust—not to life, but to death. Life was difficult, but somehow the force of life was so strong that we adjusted to it. But to cope with death, not to see in every death a scandal, was blasphemy for me. Whereas during the war, it was the most natural thing to witness other people dying. It was more natural to die than to live. So therefore we had to take all these experiences and do something with them. And this is what I'm still trying to do.

But there is no doubt, to me, anyway, that life is sacred. Death is not. And therefore, I repeat, any life is worthier, is holier, than all that has been written about life. And yet, though doctors are doing everything to prolong one's life, the minute that people become old, they're thrown away. They become useless. Then why prolong that life? To make a person ashamed and useless? There is nothing worse than to humiliate another human being. So why create conditions in which a person lives longer, only to receive humiliation?

# INTERLUDE

---

**Is there any reading of the past that would indicate that we might experience the kind of change that would be necessary for your messages to take on substance and go beyond the spirit?**

Yes and no. The same events that produce optimism are those that bring pessimism. I could tell you, for instance, about the importance of the individual. One man, and one man alone, was Mohammed or Jesus or Buddha. And the same thing could be applied to tragedies. One man began the First World War. One man was responsible for the Second World War. I think it depends on us— how we apply meaning to the word, how we use the word in order not to betray its meaning. Words can become spears, words can become rules, or words can become prayers and songs.

TEN

---

# Making Ourselves Over ...
# In Whose Image?

There are extraordinary implications for mankind in the giant strides forward that contemporary microbiology and genetics take every day in further and further identifying the very stuff of human inheritance. We're learning so fast now what we are made of. Indeed, seemingly, we soon will be able to make of ourselves what we will. Yet one wonders, "In whose image?" And about this new kind of creationism, I wonder if to you it at all feels akin to blasphemy, this making ourselves over.

First of all, can we? Is it possible for a human being to be more than human? Is it possible not to be human? Whatever we do must be measured in human terms. We are not God.

You say, "We are not God." But are we not playing God as we manipulate the genetic stuff of which we're made?

Well, that is a danger. I speak to scientists, and they like the idea that they can do things that have never been tried before. Now, I am a great admirer of medical science. The science has made extraordinary progress in the last thirty years or so. Today heart failures are no longer necessarily fatal. Cancer is not vanquished yet, but some cancers can be cured. And people have more hope because of the research being done in laboratories under medical supervision. Ethically, of course, they are correct. It is the great commandment for any human being to help another human being to live longer, better, healthier. But from there to genetic experiments is a giant step.

**You've made giant steps in your life. What is your objection to the concept of giant steps?**

Oh, wait. My giant steps, if they were giant at all, involved only myself. Maybe some of my students. Maybe some of my readers. But it's a matter of education, nothing else. I never forced anyone. I never created a situation in which people had to do what I wanted them to do. I tried to tell a few stories and repeat a few lessons that I received from my teachers.

**We were talking about power, something you would move away from.**

I don't trust power.

**Why not?**

Oh, it's too dangerous, really. Who am I to say that I know more than anyone else? That I have more right to have power? Because that's it. If you have power, that means that you believe that you are different, even superior. And therefore you may use that power. I don't think I'm superior. I don't think I'm inferior. That's not my prerogative. Nor is it my preoccupation.

But as you ask questions—and I know that you are, par excellence, the question asker—aren't you trying to move mankind in one direction or another?

One person. It's always one person.

Now, the medical researcher who is concerned with the potentially sick—what is your sense of what he's doing, by way of attempting to avoid sickness, with the manipulation of genetic materials?

What he is doing is opening a door. And who knows what lies behind that door? What I heard lately, and that of course gave me food for thought, is that in cancer research, genetic manipulation will play an important role. I cannot be against that, but I would say that the researchers should be very careful not to go too far. That is what I would say. It means setting the limits.

But these scientists are opening up, in many people's estimation, Pandora's box, to the end that mankind will be less ill. Now you say they may open doors that we do not want walked through.

Don't misunderstand. I'm not against it.

You're asking questions.

I'm asking questions. I would like scientists to ask themselves the same questions. We mustn't give up on science. I'm ignorant in matters of scientific research, really. I don't even know how to use a computer. But I would like scientists simply not to be so sure of themselves. That's all. Not to be so stubborn. I am convinced that every scientist wants to help mankind. But not to be so sure that his way is the way.

Would you really ask questions of these scientists in a way that might lead them to stop the work they've begun?

I wouldn't have them stop. But I would simply like the

scientist to see every case as unique and not say, "Because I succeeded here, next time, even if I'm not so sure, I can do it anyway."

**But certainly you and I agree that that will not happen—that in fact, given what we know about the nature of human nature and of human endeavors, once you start down a path you don't examine every case by itself. So what would you opt for?**

I would still say you should examine every case as itself. Every case is a unique case. Every human being is a unique human being, irrespective of color or ethnicity or religious belief.

Look, a surgeon who is operating on his or her patient—if for that surgeon, that patient is not the most important person in the world at that moment, that surgeon should not be there. The same should be true of the scientist. And if a scientist comes forward and says, "Look, this child is going to be born with a malfunction, and we can do something, let's do it," I would say, "Speak to the parents." The parents should ask, maybe, their spiritual leader. Who knows? But it should not be simply a matter of pushing buttons. You push a button and you have a genetic change or metamorphosis. That would lead—even if that scientist were a good person—the next generation of scientists to take it like a normal thing, like taking a cup of coffee.

**Then the question you would have a scientist put to herself or himself has to do with the morality, the appropriateness of the act about to be taken?**

And the next step. Don't forget that. What will happen then? Once it becomes routine, I'm afraid of the routine.

But then aren't you saying that's not sufficient—asking that question of myself as a scientist in relation to this particular person, this particular disease? I must be so frightened of the potential of the misuse of what I am developing—doesn't that lead to saying, "Stop the scientific procedure"?

I am afraid of something else. I am afraid that the scientist one day may say, "Actually, we can change the genes so the person will be not only a healthier but a *better* person." Which means that person will make choices in the sense of what you want him to make. That I'm afraid of. Who is making the image? That is really the person's choice. I don't want the person to lose what makes a human being noble.

Even evil?

Even his capacity for evil. I don't want the person to lose his ability to choose. Everybody chooses. We are all making choices. I don't want the scientist to prevent or to deprive me of that choice, of that ability. But in the year 2051 maybe one scientist will say, "Look, there is an area in the brain that is the moral area. Just as we know that there is an area for music. A moral area—let me manipulate it. Then we will have good people. They won't kill. They won't make war."

You're talking about fifty years or so. Don't you think that capacity to make those changes is almost upon us?

I am afraid you are right there. I simply wanted to give an illustration. Even if it happens only in the year 2051, I will be afraid of that.

We don't talk much about the Holocaust, you and I, in this context.

We can't really talk about it.

But if the manipulation of genetic materials could have prevented that manifestation of evil undreamed of before, would not this be a step and direction—

Look, if I know that one child would be saved simply because of a move by a scientist, of course I would say, "Yes, go ahead." Naturally. You are asking me a question that is painful, because you know the answer: The life of one child is more important than all the theories in the world.

Let me turn it around. During the war, important experiments were made in the camps by cruel, brutal, inhuman Nazi doctors. Maybe they discovered certain good things for human beings. Should we use them?

What I would do, of course, is do what my friend Elie Wiesel would do.

Me, I would ask a question. I feel science today has made such progress that our own scientists can make those same discoveries. There is something so ugly, so inhuman, and so dark about what those Nazi doctors did that we shouldn't benefit from it. There could be no benefit derived from that period, that tragedy. I remember somebody told me that the Pill is somehow linked to the experiments made during the war. But luckily it was discovered by our own scientists later on in a different way.

I do want to press you further on this. I appreciate what you said a moment ago about "if . . . one child would be saved," the theories would have to be moved out of the way. How do you reconcile that feeling with the hatefulness of the idea of making use of what Mengele and the others did—

They didn't discover anything that would be of use to

humanity. Let me be romantic and naive for a minute and say that these people were so evil that nothing good could come out of them. The fact is that evil does not always produce good.

**You say "does not always." I know you really mean to say "never does." But can you really mean that?**

I think so. Except, you know, in mysticism, we have certain theories that absolute evil can bring absolute good. It's a dangerous theory.

**Dangerous. So your advice to the scientist is to be careful?**

Be careful. Yes.

**And how would you formulate the question to the larger public, which actually is making choices now in many of the projects that are furthering the mapping out of our genetic content?**

Let me be romantic again. How about asking, before giving financial aid or encouragement to anyone in any level of training, for some moral guarantees? I will not give it to someone who is immoral. How about setting some rules?

**How shall we identify who will be the judge as to who is moral?**

I don't know.

**Right at this moment, mustn't there be people who will say, "What could be more immoral than to say that for a moment, scientific progress should not continue? Because we may yet alleviate pain and suffering"?**

In truth, I don't have any fixed idea about it. It is so complex. Because the Talmudic language is, "On one hand it's this, you know, on the other hand that, yet on the third hand. . . ." I cannot tell you with a perfect conviction that I know what to do. If I were president of the United States, maybe I would organize a colloquium of moral leaders, philosophers, thinkers, and poets at the White House and listen to them. I would like to listen more to the arguments.

**Do you find that we are moving closer and closer to or further and further away from that kind of moral workout?**

I think we're oscillating. Dostoevsky said, "Man is not choosing between good and evil, but he oscillates between them." And we are oscillating between a quest for absolute morality and the fear of getting it. Some people, I'm convinced, are morally dominated. They want to move toward morality. Others are not.

**But my understanding of the role of scientists, at least in the twentieth century, is that they have contributed much to man's progress but became apolitical when the application of their technology led to the destruction of six million Jews, or the coming destruction of the atmosphere, and so on.**

I'm not entirely sure I would go that far. I am also critical, as you are, and skeptical. After all, Einstein and Oppenheimer produced or helped produce an atomic bomb. And yet, after the bomb exploded both Oppenheimer and Einstein became the greatest antagonists of nuclear weapons. And they, I think, more than anyone else in the world, more than any politician, more than any moralist, managed to create an awareness of the nuclear danger.

And probably the same thing is true of many scientists today. What is it that they say about nuclear weapons? "Prometheus stole the fire from God, and we still live to regret it." But it's not entirely so, because scientists have also done great things—nuclear medicine and energy. The peaceful and useful practices of nuclear energy can offer many blessings for humankind.

**If you had to choose whether you would take the benefits of science in the twentieth century along with its atrocities, or forgo the benefits of science in the twentieth century along with its atrocities, which would you choose?**

Why must I choose? I would if I have to, which means you give me the power to choose.

**Yes, indeed. The moral power.**

Then I would say I want only the benefits but none of the threats.

**Well, I ask you to choose because we're talking less about the past and more about the future.**

If there is a future.

**You're worse than I am.**

Oh, I'm very pessimistic.

**Thanks to what men have written?**

Let's be honest. Scientists are also a product of culture. That means they are a result of what people have written. You cannot take away literature, let us say, or philosophy, or poetry, or music from the equation. If science has reached the level of quasi-perfection where it is now, it's also because of literature and philosophy and poetry. So we are all in it. You and I.

**I know you're impressed with the development of science. But there must be a cost. And I wonder what you see as that cost?**

Well, the cost is lack of ethical concerns. I would suggest a conference about the ethical need in culture today. I would like the scientists also to study humanities. I would, for instance, use all the influence that I have so that every university should have compulsory courses in the humanities—for medical students, for schools of engineering, for law schools. The lawyers should know *why* liberty is important. The doctors should know *why* life is sacred. And engineers should know *why* comfort is important for human beings.

**Do you feel that that's teachable?**

The attempt must be made. Surely it is better that the doctor reads a few books, that he goes to a few plays, that he reads a few poems under the guidance of an inspiring teacher. It's truly better to read books than not to read books; to think of culture than not to think of culture; to absorb morality, or at least examples of morality. Why? Because they need to know the meaning of it all. I like the idea, the notion, of the DNA. It means you can find, in my DNA, traces of my ancestors of two thousand years ago. That is beautiful. It's a code somehow. All we have to do is to decipher it. I am in awe, really, of the medical experiments that are being conducted to help human beings overcome sickness and disease—what doctors have done to prolong life. They have discovered in fifty years more than in the past five thousand about how to help the living. The problem is society. The moment we become old, they throw us away. At best, they send us to Miami.

**Do you respond well or poorly to the notion that in this effort to eliminate pain, suffering, evil, we are essentially denying the godhead?**

I think that if you believe in God, whatever you do is God's will. For a religious person there is no question. For a nonbeliever there is no answer. But anyone who does anything can always find the words to say, "Oh, I'm not doing it for myself. I'm doing it for something good, something noble, something sacred." Again, if one child is helped, how can you say no to that child? How can you say no to the father of the child? I really don't know what to do there. I would simply say, "Beware."

# INTERLUDE

We have assumed that as technology provides us with more and more means of simultaneously reaching so many people, we are better off for those perfected means of communication. Do you believe otherwise?

I believe otherwise, because what do we communicate? What do we say? We can say anything that can be heard millions of miles away. But what do we say to that person who is listening? What is the moral message of the last half-century? Over the last half-century, humankind has made more progress than it did during the billion years since the creation of the universe.

Material, physical, technological?

Yes, exactly. But when it comes to morality, what is the progress? Do we know more about each other than before? Do we know what's happening in somebody else's heart? Do we have more compassion for each other? Look at the homeless people here. Think of the victims of racism, the victims of discrimination, the victims of misery. Are we really better today? Have we improved in any way? Are human beings closer to one another?

# ELEVEN

# The Mystic Chords of Memory

**I have the feeling that this topic has a particularly important meaning for you.**

The word "memory" combines almost all my obsessions, all my priorities. We are committed to memory. I am because of what I remember. If I do what I do, what I'm trying to do, it's again because I remember. And therefore "memory" is probably the key word in my vocabulary.

**What are we not "memorizing"? And I use that word purposefully. What are we not committing to memory again and again that distresses you?**

I am distressed because today, memory itself, which should be a sanctuary, has become almost an abomination.

**What do you mean?**

I'll give you a very concrete example. When I went to Bosnia, I visited a prison camp. Then I understood why I remained so troubled and depressed. Not only because

I saw suffering, imprisonment, victimization. That is enough to make you feel depressed. But also because I realized that in that tormented land, it is memory that is a problem. It's because they remember what happened to their parents or their sisters or their grandparents that they hate each other.

But the reverse is also true. I believe in the redemptive quality of memory. I always try to say it's because we remember that we can be saved from further punishment. So I am saying to myself, "Maybe memory is not the answer. Not the only answer or entirely the answer." It is the main component of the answer.

**Doesn't it seem throughout history, though, that if one had to identify which aspect of memory loomed largest, it would be the negative use of memory? The hates, the grievances that are ancient?**

Yes, but then I could turn it around, you see, and say that because I remember the consequence of hate, I should teach against hate. Take religion. Religion is meant to be, after all, a link between human beings. It has become a destroyed bridge. It has become a weapon. Religions that preached love actually practiced hate. The religion that celebrated life served death. So if I then take the lessons to my students or readers, I can say, "Therefore, remember that religion must be a human experience as well. Remember that religion must bring sanctity into the profane." But it is true—we remember the negative, we remember the pain, and we stop there.

**Would you, as a consequence, embrace instead those who say, "Each day, let us begin anew"?**

No. And yet I think that memory is still the main component in human experience and any human endeavor.

Whatever we do, we must remember there is a context. There are certain words that preceded my own, certain gestures that preceded my own. There are certain adventures that preceded mine. I am a result of who knows how many generations of fathers and mothers.

**Why do you say you think of memory as redemptive? Tell me more about what you mean.**

I believe, first of all, that if we remember what human beings have done to other human beings, we can prevent other tragedies from occurring tomorrow.

**What do you base that upon? More than hope or wishful thinking?**

Understanding those evils and the consequence of those evils would also mean self-preservation. In the Holocaust, a million and a half Jewish children were killed. How many Nobel laureates among them? How many scientists, how many physicians, how many researchers? Maybe one of them or two of them or ten of them would have invented a remedy, a cure, for AIDS, cancer, heart conditions. Which means because the world—why not call it that, the world?—allowed it to happen, the world hurt itself. The world is suffering now. It's being punished.

But I don't think it deserves it, by the way, because the children of today don't deserve that punishment. They are not guilty. Surely not. Only those who committed the crimes are guilty. Only the killers are killers. And yet we suffer. So maybe this is only one example—that if we learn the lessons of the past, we would know what not to do.

**If we learn the lessons of the past, doesn't the thought occur to you that time would then stand still, would stop?**

**That we have been driven to some extent not just by the better angels of our nature but by evil, too?**

To believe that evil could disappear totally—that evil instincts would be abolished—is utopia. But I still believe that the human being is everything. I have in me everything that everybody else has. I am the totality of the human species. So are you. So is everybody else. That is the beauty about it. That means I have something of you, and you have something of me, and all of the people who read us, they may say the same thing.

Still, every human being is unique. Remember what the Nazis used to say? "What do you mean? Come on. Doctors? Jewish doctors? They are replaceable. Jewish musicians? Replaceable. Jewish scientists? Replaceable." Everybody, they thought, is replaceable. And I say no. A human being is never replaceable. Functions can be replaced. Human beings, irrespective of their color, creed, national origin, religion, are unique. That is the greatness of the human being. Once you say that, you have said everything. That means I owe something to that human being who is the center of the universe.

**Despite the beauty of your words, I ask again what indication there has been in man's long history that memory has been redemptive, that an understanding of what we have done to each other has stopped us from doing the same thing again and again.**

I can't give you evidence, really. It's an instinctive hope, perhaps, or a faith, a trust that I've placed in ourselves. Maybe it's unfounded. But what is the alternative? What else will save the human condition? What else will save humanity? We have seen (I can now plead your case) that in spite of two thousand years of Western civilization, in spite of all the great musicians in Germany—the Bachs and the Beethovens—and all the poets—the Schillers—and the philosophers—the Fichtes and the Kants—what has happened in Berlin? So you may say, "Look, we remember them. We study them in school. After all, who can study philosophy without studying Kant? And who can love music without adoring Bach and Beethoven? And yet look—it ended up in Auschwitz." So this is, of course, a case in point.

But I must say "and yet": And yet what I can do then is take that paradigmatic event and turn it around and say that until now we have not succeeded. But because we have reached a paradigmatic, paroxysmal state of affairs in evil and suffering and death, we must turn history around. And from that memory you must draw sustenance. Memory is my homeland. It can protect me. In fact, it did.

**What do you mean?**

I would have gone insane—not during, but after the war. I would have lost my mind or my life. And it is because I remembered that I could remain human.

**Remembered what?**

The good and the bad. In memory, you are not alone. You are surrounded by people. Some of those are not here anymore, naturally, but they are in your memory. They live. And you hear them and you speak to them, and when you need a presence, it's their presence. Of course, it's a dead presence, but still it's a presence. The presence of the dead is also a presence. And what is worse than to live without a future? It's to live without a past.

The first question that in the Talmudic tradition a

person should ask himself or herself is, "Where do I come from?" You know, you have visited with me. And you saw behind my desk there is always a picture of the house where I was born. In the beginning it had no electricity. Even to the end it didn't have running water. I want to remember that is the place where I come from. Whenever I see important people, I must remember where I come from. If not, I wouldn't be able to write what I am writing.

**You said that if you hadn't had memory during the time in the camp and afterward, you would not have survived.**

And I think the Jewish people wouldn't have survived, either. The Jewish people would have gone under long ago. Logically, we shouldn't have continued. There wasn't a century during which the Jewish people have not been persecuted by somebody for some reason. And I think if we remain, it's because we have memory. We remember the Exodus, we remember moral values, a moral mission, perhaps. That doesn't make us, by the way, superior, you know. I reject any notion of religious triumphalism or nationalistic or ethnic or racial superiority. But there is something that brought drama in our history—that memory. The moment you invoke memory, there is drama.

**At the end of the war, what was left in terms of your childhood devotion to religion and to religious tradition?**

In 1945, when I came to France, to a children's home, I "rebecame" religious, just as before. When I think about it now, I don't understand it. It was as if I wanted to close the brackets. I picked up the Talmud—exactly at the page where I had left it. I wanted to become—to "rebecome"— exactly the same adolescent, or even more religious.

**Did it work?**

For a few years, I wanted so much to think that if my studies could become parentheses, all that happened actually didn't happen. And I would wake up, and my parents, my teachers, and my friends would be there. Then, when I began studying philosophy, I found the tools for my questioning. But the question remained, the quest remains. And I know that whatever I do will be mutilated always, because of that breakdown in the 1940s. Whatever I will do as an individual, in my prayers, or in my dreams, or in my work, will never be satisfactory.

**What have you done with those parentheses? I have always been curious about how you dealt with what happened to you, to your parents, to your family, how you dealt with it in terms of your religion, and the question that you asked yourself: Could there be a God?**

You know very well that all the questions I had remained open. I found no answer. However, certain principles apply. I don't believe that because I suffered I have the right to inflict suffering.

**What do you mean, "inflict suffering"?**

I mean to make other people suffer or to justify suffering, by diminishing, by opposing, or by hating other people's suffering. I don't believe that because I went through certain experiences it is the fault of Abraham and Isaac and Jacob. I may have my problems, and I do, with the master of the universe, but why should I say that my tradition is responsible for them? And therefore I am profoundly involved in study. That has been my passion. As I've said, what saved my sanity not during but after the war was my passion for study.

The question is really not how we survived the war, but how we survived mentally afterward, when we came out and we saw that life was business as usual and how very few people cared. That was the great disillusionment. When I realized for the first time that Roosevelt knew what was happening to us, I cannot tell you the despair that was mine. In my little town, we loved Roosevelt. He was seen as a surrogate father of my people. We recited prayers for him. Yet the indifference of the United States leadership to the suffering of the Jewish people in Europe is unforgivable.

**What was that due to, a lack of information?**

Oh no, knowledge was here.

**Then what?**

I don't know. People who were here tell me that there was so much anti-Semitism then, somehow Roosevelt had to take it into account—he was afraid of acting too aggressively in order not to antagonize the electorate. I am told that even the Congress was against immigration. But all these reasons are practical reasons, and I do not accept them. We knew some twenty or thirty years ago that Roosevelt and the military and political leadership, including the Jewish leadership of this country, knew everything about what was going on in Europe. In America, they knew about Auschwitz in 1942. I, who was in Hungary, didn't. And in 1944, when Hungarian Jews came to Auschwitz, they didn't know what it was. Had they known, many of us would have escaped. The Russians were fifteen or twenty miles away. How can anyone explain that to me? I don't know. The information was here. But somehow it did not become knowledge. It was one thing to know that Jews were being killed, and another to know that something had to be done for them. And those two zones were separate. I still don't understand how it happened, why it happened. It was totally, totally insane. History went mad.

**What do you mean by that?**

It could have been avoided. The greatest tragedy in recorded history could have been avoided. It would have taken so little, really, to stop Hitler. And I don't understand the victims. Really, I don't understand them. They became perfect victims, just as the killers were perfect killers. I don't understand the indifference surrounding the killers and the victims. In the *New York Times* of those days, the first stories about the Holocaust were buried in inside pages. By the way, the *Times* had the courage under Punch Sulzberger to have an exhibit in the New York Public Library where they did say they failed with regard to the Holocaust. What does it mean that people were capable of committing such atrocities? Theologically, I don't understand it either. Where was God? There is so much I don't understand. But there are people who do, by the way. Who say so at least.

**Who?**

Oh, I've seen explanations in many books. Philosophers and theologians and psychologists and psychiatrists and sociologists all have explanations. I find them, let's say, not satisfactory.

**Why? Because you won't accept their basic assumptions about the nature of human nature?**

Because I don't think there is an answer. Maybe God can give an answer, and even if God gave me the answer, I wouldn't accept it. If God performed a miracle by saving some, that means he refused to perform miracles in condemning the others. I don't go for that.

**Then why do you say "I don't understand" if you're really saying "Don't explain it, I won't accept it"?**

Suppose there's a prophet who would come down. Granted, there are no prophets anymore, since the destruction of the first temple, twenty-five hundred years ago. But suppose God were to choose a prophet and say, "Okay, you are my prophet now, Isaiah. Go back and tell your people what happened and why." I would like to meet him. Because he was a prince of prophets, as we called him. But I think he would say, "No, the death of six million children, parents, grandparents cannot have an answer. Not even from God."

**In your novel *The Forgotten*, when you address yourself to your protagonist, you write, "Was it his wish that my memory substitute for his own? That I do the remembering for him? Is that even possible?" And I think that's a question about what you are doing for us. Is it possible for your memory and the memory of your son, in turn, and of the rest of us, to substitute for the experience of the Holocaust?**

No. The experience remains unique. But the memory of it is not. You will never know what I know—in a way I don't want you to know—because that knowledge would mean an experience, an experience such as the one that I have known. But the memory of that knowledge can be used. So I try to share with you not my experience, but the memory that I carry within myself. I would believe that anyone who listens to a witness becomes a witness. So all those who are our students, our children, our children's children, and who listen to our tale, become custodians of that tale.

**Yet at the end of *The Forgotten*, it seems to me that you question whether memory, and the imposition of that memory upon those to come, is possible, is fair.**

It is a terrible dilemma. Because on the one hand I would like you to remember; on the other hand, I know you cannot remember. *I* cannot remember.

**What do you mean, *you* cannot remember?**

I don't remember everything. I tried, even during the war, as a child, as an adolescent, to see as much as possible. To see faces, to remember gestures, to see the suffering, the resistance to the suffering, the resistance to evil, and evil itself. I didn't know that I would survive the war, but I somehow, as a Jew, as a human being, felt that as long as I was alive, I must remember life. But now, I wonder, what about those whom I have not managed to recall, to gather in my memory? I see hundreds of people, thousands of people, anonymous, wanderers in the night, going to the flames. I don't remember all of them. So what about those whom only I have seen? What about the words that nobody uttered? The thoughts, the prayers, the hopes, the despairing calls for meaning? That is my despairing fight.

**"Despairing fight" . . . isn't that a contradiction in terms?**

Oh, yes, but I'm not against contradictions. You know that; life is a contradiction. But what I would not like to have is a contradiction that turns against our fellow human brothers, companions, sojourners. The moment a contradiction turns against humanity, I discard it.

**You've always said, "Lest we forget." Yet at the end of *The Forgotten* you raise the question as to whether it is possible. And if it is possible, what then do we do with the most enormous event of the century? Do we forget it?**

Even if you remember a spark of the flame, it's enough. Even if you remember one face, it would be enough. But always remember it's only one face multiplied by six million. What I try to do is to bring you closer to the gate, and I tell you you cannot go beyond that—that only those who were there know what it was being there. But come closer . . . and the only way to come closer is to come closer to my memory, meaning to the memory of those who survived the war and that event. Testimonies, prayers, meetings, words, silences . . . every person has his or her own way of expressing what nobody can ever express—the ineffable experience. Supposedly only God's name is ineffable, but it's not so. Our experience, too, is ineffable.

Look, do I remember the Inquisition? To the Jewish people, it was a tremendous event. We remember it. I remember it because I studied Jewish history. And I am fascinated with all the elements that play a role in Jewish history. Why are we hated? Why were we hated so persistently, consistently, by so many people?

**Why?**

I tell you the truth: I don't want to give them an answer. Let those who hate answer you.

**Fair enough.**

I don't want to help them. Let them invent a good answer. If they have a good answer, fine. I don't think they have one. But the fact is that for two thousand years, we Jews have suffered. We were either too poor or too rich; either too religious or not enough; either too patriotic or too cosmopolitan; either Communist or anti-Communist. And then all the contradictions merged into hatred of the Jew. It was possible to say something and believe in the opposite and hate a Jew. Why? That fascinates me. So I try to understand the Inquisition in the name of love, of God, of mercy. Priests, after all, who served their savior, thinking that they would please the savior and God, brought Jews to the stake and watched. Do you know that they had a handbook in the Inquisition on how to torture? And it had the imprimatur of the Vatican.

So, because I'm interested, somehow I remember the Inquisition. I hope that five hundred years from now there will still be a planet and society and human beings who will remember our tragedy. After all, we Jews remember what happened four thousand years ago. We left Egypt. We sit down every Passover and we celebrate because we say, "As if we had left Egypt." We fast to commemorate the destruction of the temple. And come on, that happened in 586 B.C. Why are we doing it today?

**Do I misunderstand? When we first met, perhaps two decades ago, the concern that memory will not be retained—at least insofar as the Holocaust was concerned—was very real in your mind.**

It still is in a way, of course. But don't forget that for the last twenty years, certain things have been attempted. Books have been written in the hundreds by survivors and by victims whose manuscripts were found. And there are museums in Washington and in New York. All over the world now there is such a gigantic effort being made to help memory. So I'm less pessimistic than I was twenty years ago.

**Then how do you explain the growing sense in this country that the dimensions of the Holocaust were so much less than we have known them to be in the past?**

In the beginning, people didn't want to know. Then they didn't want to believe it. It is human to refuse to believe that human beings could be so inhuman, because it threatens everybody. Therefore they invented all kinds of escapism. One of them was, for instance, an abstraction: saying Auschwitz represented man's inhumanity to man. It's wrong. It's also that, but Auschwitz meant the murder of hundreds and thousands and millions of people, human beings who were alive and who no longer are. You can't reduce such an agony, such a mystery, to an abstraction: "man's inhumanity to man."

And then the next phase was, here in America especially, the "embellishment"—meaning even death can be embellished. Death is an industry in America. Everything is beautiful. The funeral in America is a beautiful program. It shouldn't be. Death is a brutal phenomenon. You shouldn't put makeup on the person who dies, or on the whole ceremony. And therefore some people took the Holocaust and made it such an event too. They made it commercial, they made it kitsch—why not say it?—kitsch. They trivialized it. In doing so, I think, they caused great harm and prejudice to memory.

**And how do you account for the increasing nativism that is connected with an outright denial of the Holocaust?**

It's not a huge group. It's a very small, marginal, very well financed group. I don't know who gives them the money. But one must be evil or insane, really, to propose anything like that. They are the most vicious anti-Semites in history in claiming that we did not lose our parents, that we did not see what we have seen, that we did not endure what we have endured. And I don't think that the American people or anyone else really lends credence to their silly, ugly, stupid arguments. It's so ugly that to argue with them, or to refute them is unworthy. I would never grant them the dignity of a debate.

**So you are not terribly concerned about that.**

Not about them. But because of time, people forget. After all, it's normal. The fourth or fifth generation will know less than we do.

**But are you hopeful or otherwise when it comes to our remembering what happened in the thirties and the forties?**

To tell you the whole truth, I'm really desperate. I force myself to be hopeful because there is an assault on Jewish memory, more than before.

**On Jewish memory?**

Mainly on Jewish memory of the Holocaust. There isn't a week, almost, without a book coming out somehow to attack it. I'm not speaking about the deniers. I let them be. I let them silence themselves with their own shame. But there are people—scholars, historians—who discredit the survivors' legitimacy, the survivors as witnesses, by saying that they are too subjective, too involved. And also in some cases, you know, memories are not as faithful as they used to be, and because of that there could be here and there some minor, minor discrepancies. Then they say the whole testimony is worthless. Many of us feel assaulted.

**Where do the assaults come from?**

I won't give you the names, because I don't want to involve myself in that, but there are those who write, let's say, that one problem is that we use the Holocaust for Israel. Another says the Holocaust has replaced the Jewish religion in America—that the Jew now defines himself or herself only because of the Holocaust.

And then they show, for instance, silly things. After the Eichmann trial there was a trial in Frankfurt of Auschwitz guards. But if it hadn't been for the Eichmann trial, there would have been nothing else. The German government didn't care, really. Where were the guards found? In the phone book. They didn't even hide. The SS guards at Auschwitz were listed in the phone book. They went back to their homes, the pharmacist to his drugstore, and the baker to his bakery.

And they would come every day to the court. And they would laugh, every day. Every day they'd laugh. For them it was a farce. There was something of farce in all that. For instance, let's say witnesses would identify a guard. They would be asked, "You remember him? Where did you see him in Auschwitz? What day did you see him? Was it Monday or Friday?" And then they would say, "Tell me, what was the color of his belt on that Monday? And how many buttons?" And of course it was forbidden during the war for Jews to look at the SS in their eyes. You would die for looking. Yet the witness had to remember how many buttons there were. And therefore there were inconsistencies and the haters would laugh. So when you bring all this together, I fear there is an assault.

**What are your feelings on teaching the Holocaust?**

I'm for teaching. When I began my academic career at City College, at least one of the two courses I gave was on the Holocaust, because very few people at that point taught it. I was persuaded to do it. For two years, it was the most difficult thing to do.

**For you, personally?**

Personally. I have such a gratitude and admiration for those who do teach the Holocaust, because I cannot. It was difficult to be with students in class and read to them about Warsaw or about Treblinka. The students couldn't leave; nor could I. So it was harrowing. But I think the most important lessons could be taught in that environment.

**And eventually by people who did not experience the Holocaust?**

Certainly. Most of the people who teach it now haven't experienced it. But they are good professors and they are committed. If one can teach the Holocaust without trembling, one shouldn't teach it. And most of the people who teach that subject tremble—before, during, and after. And that trembling they have inherited from us.

**So in the twenty-first century, this extraordinary event will still exist?**

It will exist in the testimonies, in the chronicles, in the documents. Not in fiction. I think a book of fiction cannot reveal the truth of that period. Literature and Auschwitz do not go together.

**Well, what about the Muses, the rivalry between history and literature?**

History and literature, of course, are part of our experiences, our intellectual endeavor. One cannot live outside history and one cannot live without literature. The problem is, what is more important, memory or fiction? What should be the predominant element in our endeavor, in our quest? Memory without fiction, I would accept. Fiction without memory, no, I would not.

**But my understanding is that colleagues of yours who celebrate literature and who want to commemorate the Holocaust do not do so without memory, but feel rather that fiction is a way of preserving memory better than we ourselves can preserve it, because you and I are simply mortal.**

We are indeed. Either I believe that memory must be truthful but is not always, or I believe that fiction, because of its artistic truths, is more truthful than memory. Can they go together? I don't think so. And yet I know that certain attempts have been made by great writers, and some have succeeded. It is possible. I cannot do it. Nobody can imagine what Auschwitz was unless one was there. Only those who were there know what it was. So therefore there's a limit there already. What the enemy has done is create a place of evil and cruelty and death of such magnitude that we cannot grasp it now.

Now, we can remember fragments. They of course offer us an assurance that the Holocaust will not be forgotten. The danger is in trivialization. It can be trivialized, it can be cheapened, and it has been done. I am not a censor; I would never say that a person is not free to do whatever he or she wants in literature. But I simply cannot do it.

**I recall that some years back, you were so despairing of the effectiveness—or ineffectiveness—of the television series "Holocaust." Your concern was that that nightmare had become an entertainment.**

Absolutely. It became a trivialized experience because of its superficiality. The common denominator was so low that people loved seeing Auschwitz as a love story—a cheap love story at that. And you know very well that each segment had to be cut into twelve minutes for the commercials, and therefore the laughter had to be in its place and the tears in their place. I think those programs did more harm than we know.

**But what chance is there that without the aid of imagination, history really will survive? Where will it survive if not in the mortal minds of the colleagues who experienced it with you?**

It can survive; it already has survived. This is the most documented tragedy in recorded history. We have in our possession elements given to us by the victims themselves—by children and by the old, by agnostics and by the faithful, even by the killers—in pictures, in words, in poetry, in music. Millions of pieces of evidence exist now. And they are available to anyone who wants to know. Therefore, I am not afraid, really, of forgetting. The event cannot be erased. The problem, of course, is the embellishment. If an event is embellished to an extent that the inner truth—not only the artistic truth—is gone, what remains?

**You're saying there's no way once the embellishment begins—**

—to go back to the soul. What can we do then?

**And yet memory is not pure. It needs to be interpreted. When Daniel Goldhagen argues that the Holocaust would not have been possible without the encouragement of a substantial portion of so-called ordinary Germans, he is expressing ideas that have been challenged by others who are as concerned as he is about the Holocaust.**

That's all right. If the historians quarrel, that's natural. But when the historian quarrels with the novelist, then it's a problem. Even more so when an historian or a novelist is quarreling with a witness. Then I would always favor the witness. Even if the testimony given by the witness is partially faulty, I would say the witness is right.

I was telling my students the other day the perhaps apocryphal story of Abraham Lincoln being introduced to Harriet Beecher Stowe, the author of *Uncle Tom's Cabin*, and saying to her, "So you're the little lady who wrote the book that made this great war." When you talk as you do, I can't help thinking about the power of literature to rouse our emotions, to rouse our determination. Yet you fear novelization as trivialization ultimately because it is not limiting itself to history, to fact.

I'm a novelist, so of course I believe in literature. However, what I'm afraid of is when novels will be seen as documents. That is my fear. It's like the United States Holocaust Memorial Museum in Washington, in which I invested so many years of my life. If a person goes to a museum, leaves, and says, "Now I know," I have failed. If a person leaves the museum after hours and hours of visiting and learning and says, "Now I don't know," then I know I have succeeded. Same as writing a novel. If the novel says, "Now go and read the documents, read the testimonies," then it's perfect. But if the novel comes instead of the documentation, then it's not.

I know that at the two-day Boston University symposium in honor of your seventieth birthday, there was a disagreement on this subject. How did it work itself out?

It was only one session. It worked itself out because both sides were superbly eloquent and articulate. But one side was saying, "The novelist has all the rights in the world." And you are not talking about rights, are you? You're talk-

ing about wrongs, really. That a novel becomes, by definition, wrong.

If the goal of that novel is not to convey history, then it's
all right. But if the novelist says, "The goal of this novel
is to present history," then it's wrong. Not only that.
Suppose a brilliant novelist decides to write a novel describing how the Holocaust didn't occur? What then?
The main thing that I really objected to with "Holocaust" was the fact that the television series was presented as a documentary. Had it been presented simply
as a show, well, I wouldn't have liked it, but I would not
have criticized it since I really don't like to criticize. I like
to celebrate. Whenever I write a review of a book, it must
be to celebrate. Why should I be the one to mete out punishment to a writer or to an artist or to a poet?

On the other hand, I see students who read a page of
testimony. They are more deeply moved than by the best
novel that they could read.

**Certainly, visiting the Holocaust Memorial Museum in
Washington was, for me, the most moving experience I've
ever had. And those shoes, victim's shoes . . . I don't know
why the shoes stayed in my mind. They cannot be eradi-
cated.**

Of course not. But I think the best—the most human—
experience that one should feel is if one visits Birkenau,
in Poland. It's not a museum, just barracks. Go there.
Something remains in the air, in the clouds. More than a
million people were killed there. To be there, it's more
than all the museums in the world. But be warned: To
visit Birkenau is heartbreaking, more than any novel in
the world. And the same is true for testimonies. No nov-

elist has the power, the pathos, and the dark beauty of a young boy's desire to survive, in his words.

**So you really hope that the Holocaust stays "off limits."**

I don't even dare to say that because it would sound as if I want to censor or limit the novelist's right. No. I would like the novelist to be sensitive to our concerns, even when he or she writes the novel.

**Now, you can deal with all this because you are a man of the world. You reach out. What about other survivors? Those who wanted memory, as you have stressed, and who now themselves must prepare to be no more as the years bring them so much closer to the end of their lives?**

It's true; it's the end of an era, the end of our generation. That is my anguish. Soon the last survivor will be gone. And then what? I used to say that in the beginning, survivors went to weddings, then to circumcision ceremonies, then to the children's weddings. Now we go to funerals. And the community is shrinking. We are an endangered species. What do we do? We try to build a sanctuary within that memory. And to give our life to it.

When I wrote my very first book, it was ten years after the war. My principal goal, really, was to reach the survivors, my peers. Why? Because in the beginning they didn't talk. They didn't talk because nobody wanted to hear them. And I wanted to show them, "Look, it's possible to talk, and even if it isn't, we must talk." So my goal was to inspire them—"Look what I am doing."

I didn't succeed in the beginning. It took years and years and years of work to convince them that every one of them is a witness and everyone's testimony is uniquely qualified and uniquely needed. Now there are many of them who write books. I get so many manuscripts, and you know, I try to help everyone. I write forewords and last words and epilogues and blurbs. For a document of that caliber, of that kind of nature, I'm ready to do anything.

So now they do speak. As I said, students came to me when I was teaching at City College. And all of a sudden I realized that most of them were children of survivors. And then I realized they came to me because their parents didn't talk to them. I became a surrogate father. Then the parents came to me, and I became to them a surrogate son—a bridge between the father and the son. And it was very moving to try to tell the children, "You now become the parents of your parents. They see in you their own parents, and you must help them more than they can help you."

**In what way is that help most needed now?**

I have said it so many times: To forget the victims means to kill them a second time. We couldn't prevent the first killing, but we are responsible for the second one if it takes place. If there was one basic obsession that was common to all the victims, it was not to allow the world to forget what had happened. And that is our responsibility. I also believe that although the event was a Jewish event, a Jewish tragedy, it had universal implications and applications. If we were to forget what happened to the Jewish people, then other things could happen to other people. Which means that I don't want my past to become somebody else's future. And that is really why we write, why we teach, why we do what we are doing— trying to maintain a memory which is a memory of flame and of despair and of death and of hunger and humiliation.

**But when you write, "Don't tell your son and don't tell your father that we must belong to the world at large, that we must transcend ourselves by supporting all causes and fighting for the victims of every injustice," that struck me as so quintessentially *not* the Elie Wiesel I have known.**

It's true, but the character of the novel has to say it. It's apt for him, not for me. I believe we must transcend, provided we remain who we are. What I mean to say is, don't give up your Jewishness in order to become universal. The only way for me to become universal is through my Jewishness. I do fight for other causes; I always have. My life is testimony to that, and I am still fighting, be it for the minorities in America, Indian or African-American, the victims of apartheid in South Africa, or whatever. I try to help, modestly, because I don't have that much power—except the power, occasionally, of some of my words.

But I cannot allow my Jewishness to be wiped out in exchange for something I would do for others. I don't want to do that. If I were to kill the Jew in me, what would I do? I would actually do what Hitler did, on a different scale. And for that and for other reasons, I love my Jewishness. I love the traditions I have inherited, I love the moral precepts that I'm learning every day. But when I say that, I mean that a Christian may say the same thing. I allow him to feel the same way about his or her Christianity as I feel about my Jewishness, or as the Muslim feels about Islam. I believe in tolerance, but tolerance means I accept you for what you are. I don't want you to change. I don't want you to resemble me. I don't need another me. That's what I meant.

**And how does that relate to your feelings about assimilation?**

I'm against assimilation. Not only for Jews but for anyone.

**You're against it?**

Of course I'm against assimilation. I'm for integration, meaning the legal integration of a community, meaning that we are all equally entitled to the same rights and the same duties. A Jew or Buddhist or Muslim or black or Hispanic—it doesn't matter. They are all the same. But as a person, as an individual, why give up a heritage that is thirty-five hundred years old? In this country, we celebrated together the bicentennial of the Constitution. Why? Because this is a living document and the society is living by its spirit. The Bible is thirty-five hundred years old, and to some people it is still a living document. I always think about it. You know, we are proud of Lincoln, who abolished slavery. Well, we abolished slavery three thousand years ago. The first law after the Ten Commandments is against slavery. Now, why give that up? It is foolish for a writer, for an artist, for a musician, to give up such sources and resources. There is so much in them, such an inspiration, such a wealth of ideas and sensitivities and memories.

**Why do you define assimilation as giving all of that up?**

Because that is the meaning of assimilation to me, at least.

**Do you think it need be?**

What else could it mean? I'm speaking about the Bible—

meaning the Jewish tradition, Jewish history, Jewish
consciousness, which to me is not opposed to a universal
consciousness. Quite the opposite. I repeat: a Jew can attain universality through his or her Jewishness, and that
the aim, really, is to attain universality through that consciousness. And that goes for a Christian or for anyone
else. Assimilation, in my vocabulary, means to give up
the heritage, to change everything, to change the name,
to change religion, or to change tradition. And that, I
feel, is foolish.

**You talk about making tradition survive. Do you dis-
tinguish between "good" traditions and those that have
proved to be more divisive, more dangerous to our survival?**

I'm sure there are traditions that do carry in them and
with them violence and hatred. And of course I oppose
them. My goal as an educator is to show that some traditions are more human than others. But I would never say
that mine are superior to any other.

**But you want to foster, to preserve, the great traditions?**

No other religious tradition has been as threatened, as
assaulted, as endangered as ours. Show me one. We are
the only tradition of antiquity that survived antiquity.

**But there are those who say, "My country, right or wrong."
Are you saying, "My religion, right or wrong"?**

No, of course not. My people carried our little book in
exile, from one exile to another, for two thousand years.
We didn't carry money. We had no treasures. We had the
Book, which kept us alive for two thousand years. And
out of this book emerged other books. So we became so
centered that the danger was in ignoring others, other
traditions.

There are certain elements in my religion that are wrong. That I try to fight. There is now a small segment in Israel that is racist, which embarrasses me as a Jew. I don't know whether they and I belong to the same people, whether they and I claim kinship with the same tradition. Jews can be racist. But they're not Israel. They are a small segment. I believe the Jewish tradition is one of compassion.

**In "When Hatred Seized the Nation," your article about the Dreyfus affair, you wrote, "I cannot conclude this text without recalling Theodor Herzl, who as a correspondent for a Viennese newspaper in France witnessed the ceremony in which Dreyfus was degraded. He heard the shouts of the anti-Semites crying out for death. It was at this point, according to the legend, that the assimilated writer decided that assimilation was not a valid theory. It was at this point that he decided to found the Zionist movement. In the midst of an anti-Semitic nightmare he began to dream of a Jewish state." Now, you are doing more than concluding the piece there.**

Of course. I celebrate Jewish history there. It has extraordinary imagination and sometimes a sense of irony. Here you have a meeting, or nonmeeting, between two assimilated Jews, who wanted nothing better than to be assimilated and accepted by the Gentile society around them. Herzl was an assimilated Jew who worked for a very famous newspaper from Vienna. Dreyfus didn't even know that he was prosecuted as a Jew, which is the irony of it all. And yet, there was that moment of encounter and two assimilated Jews meet and the result is a Jewish state. And I find it extraordinary.

There is a marvelous anecdote I must tell you: Sigmund Freud was from Vienna, Theodor Herzl was from Vienna. Apparently both of them lived on the same street, a few houses apart, at the same time. And they never met. Now, imagine Theodor Herzl knocking on the door and saying, "Dr. Freud, I have a dream."

**Do you think it was a dream that should have been realized or analyzed?**

Oh, if I had a choice, of course realized. For two thousand years we were waiting for that dream. It had to come from an assimilated Jew.

**What has happened lately to the emotions, the concerns, of the Jewish community in this country in terms of assimilation?**

Well, I think things haven't changed much. There are Jewish writers, as there are other writers, who don't know much about their own heritage. There are some Jewish writers who don't know anything about Judaism except what they read in others' work. In other words, if I were a French writer, would I write if I didn't know Victor Hugo or Rabelais or Racine or Montaigne? I think a Jewish writer should know, in text, the basic treasures of our heritage. I would very much like to bring about a situation in which we would go back to the authenticity of our very being. And to be authentic, I must first of all be who I am and what I am. Which means I am the sum total of thousands of scholars and disciples. That gives me a very special feeling—that when I study and when I teach, I feel that I have people looking over my shoulders, meaning Abraham is looking there and listening. What am I saying in his name, or Moses'? These are all giants in human history.

**But doesn't that kind of authenticity, as you so lovingly call**

it, enter into tension with—or, to put it more baldly, conflict with—the notion of universality?

Not at all. Universality today . . . could it exclude Abraham, or Moses, or Plato?

Let me then ask you perhaps a more difficult question.
Given modern technology, given the fact that our world is
made smaller and smaller by it, do you think that we will
further accept the idea of universality?

I think that the age of communication, which is ours, is
extraordinary. We have made such progress in that area. I
remember when the first man was on the moon, I was
much more struck and astonished and grateful to hear
him than to know about the scientific achievement
that put him there. To put him there meant nothing to
me, but when he talked, I could hear a communication
between the man on the moon and the man on earth. It
was a great moment.

You know, Buddha, Plato, Jeremiah, and Lao-tzu
were almost contemporaries, and they didn't know
about one another. So imagine if you could bring them
together before a television camera. If we had such a
program, what it would do for humankind! Now we
can do that. You can bring together scholars, poets, and
scientists from all the horizons, all the spheres, and establish an exchange, a dialogue, a multi-dialogue. It's
possible, and beneficial.

And do you think the words uttered in those ancient times
were qualitatively different from what we say to each other
today?

Oh, they were so much better. Whatever I have to say
today, the words are not mine. I take them from the
prophets, from the ancient masters. Nothing I could say

could even come close to the intensity, to the beauty, let alone the truth, of a prophet or an ancient philosopher in Greece.

I feel those words are here. They are here as the mountains are here, as the clouds are here, as the air is here. And we integrate ourselves in them. If they could survive three thousand years, that means that there is something in their presence. And it's a privilege for us to be part of their landscape.

# INTERLUDE

───────────

You know, when I finish a book, I am not satisfied. A friend of mine, Piotr Rawicz, who wrote a great novel, told me once that when he finished, he felt the taste of ashes in his mouth. And so do I. It's never satisfactory. If I write a story, and it's filled with despair, I don't give it to my publisher until I find a way out. If despair were my only lesson, I think I would keep it in my drawer. There must be something else. I don't want young people to read only about despair.

---

# TWELVE

# Anti-Semitism

What do you think about the recent nationwide sur-
vey conducted by the Anti-Defamation League that found
17 percent of Americans, or about 35 million adults,
holding views about Jews that are "unquestionably anti-
Semitic"? George Will probably put it most succinctly in
saying that anti-Semitism is the world's most durable ideology, and once again it is seemingly flourishing throughout Europe, as well as much of the rest of the world. What
is your response to these figures and this talk? What's
happening?

Well, like you, I am astonished, dismayed. Even more
than that, I am angry. But what can one do? Anti-
Semitism is the oldest group prejudice in history. So
many "isms" have vanished, were defeated, but anti-
Semitism is still here. Nazism was defeated, fascism vanquished, communism discredited. Anti-Semitism is still
around. And you wonder why.

After the war, the anti-Semites didn't dare reveal themselves. It was unfashionable. Everybody thought, Well, who wants to be seen in the company of those who created those places of curse, malediction, and death? Now, three generations later, people already feel they can drop the mask.

The anti-Semites don't understand. They refuse to understand that here is a people who for 4,000 years, at least, carried on a certain mission—of bringing awareness into the world, of conscience, of trying to help each other. And they don't understand why we want to do that. We have suffered so much, from so many quarters, for so many reasons.

**But why focus on the Jews?**

Ah, if I knew. We have been asked this question for thousands of years, and we still don't know the answer. People ask, "Why did God choose you?" Well, *did* God choose us? Ask God. Let Him answer. I have no authority to answer for Him. Others ask, "Since God chose you, why aren't you worthy of God's trust?" That expresses the religious hatred. And then there is the economic hatred and the political hatred and the ethnic hatred and the cultural hatred, and all of these hatreds are again somehow focused on us.

**As always, there is this question to which there is no response. And yet, how do we answer our children? How do we explain anti-Semitism to our children, to those who come after us?**

Occasionally I am asked, "Why do so many people hate you? There must be something about you that elicits their hatred." And I say, Why should I make their work easier? Ask the anti-Semites. Let them reply. And then I may have answers to their answers. I may refute them; I may reject them. Often, I feel I do not wish to dignify them with an answer.

**In the 1950s I did a television series on anti-Semitism. And there seemed then to be a very real need on the part of my guests to say, "Don't ever think that this is a Jewish problem. It is a problem of the anti-Semite, not of the Semite." Nonetheless, here we are, suffering, and we will suffer more.**

Yes, it was the haters' problem then, it is their problem now. We are only the victims of that problem if we choose to be victims. We are not victims. We can fight back. We have words. We have ways of explaining what we want to explain, refuting what we want to refute, and affirming what we want to affirm. After all, I do not consider myself a victim. I used to be one, during the war, but not afterward. So they want us to be victims, but we are not. Not only are we not their victims, we are their judges. And this bothers them. We judge haters.

**You say, "We judge haters." What judgment do you make? That they are sick? That they are poor? That they are oppressed? That they are ignorant?**

I remember a discussion I once had with some, let's say, important people. And there was an African-American lady who down deep was really on our side. We were fighting for the same causes against the same enemies. And at one point, because of some ugly incident between Blacks and Jews in Williamsburg, in New York, she said, "But you must understand these people because, after all, all the Jews are so rich." And I said, "Really, are all the Jews rich? I can take you this afternoon to Brooklyn, I will show you how some Jews live there. I will show you families of seven who live in an apartment of two rooms, and who have nothing to eat, except what they receive, either from the community or the government. I will show you that." You cannot say the Jews are this or that. We have our own poor, our own rich, our own good people, our own bad people.

**But, as a people, is it appropriate for us to make others' attitudes toward Israel a kind of litmus test when it comes to our concerns about anti-Semitism? Must we consider someone who is opposed to Israel an anti-Semite?**

I don't. If a person has shown by example that he or she praises Israel, when Israel is worthy of praise, but now says, "Look, I don't agree with what Mr. This or General That is doing," then he has the right to be critical. Because of my past and my life, I cannot simply criticize. I am not that harsh. I try to give Israel every chance. It's a young nation, which was born out of an ancient people. It has some attenuating circumstances, which are understandable. If others are more critical, okay. But if somebody always criticizes Jews has always done so, will always do so, obviously, that person is an anti-Semite.

**Do you think we're running into the danger of blaming, or labeling as anti-Semitic, individuals who are simply opposed to the idea of a Jewish state?**

Oh, I couldn't conceive of anyone today who remembers the past and is intelligent and knows history who would say that. Look, a Jewish state was born three years after Auschwitz. If that state had been postponed fifty years, or a hundred years, the Jewish people might not have survived. Now Israel's existence is linked to the Jewish people's existence all over the world. So, inevitably, anyone who opposes Israel's existence is an anti-Semite—basically, he opposes Jewish lives *in* Israel.

**How would you have Israel respond to the threats against it?**

The first objective must be the end of the suicide killings. If I had my way—and I've suggested this to somebody who could actually implement it—I would convene a meeting of the highest spiritual authorities of Islam. I would urge them to issue a fatwa saying, "Look, you Palestinians are patriots. We admire you for that. You want to fight for a homeland. We will help you. But there is one limit that you must impose by yourself—no suicide killing. That's against the Koran, it's against civilization, it's against humanity." I think that would help. Once that happens, everything is possible.

**How do you reply to those who say that is not possible, because the Palestinians and those around them will simply not accept Israel's existence, and that ultimately there will be an attempt once again to drive Israel into the sea?**

Oh, I too feel it very often, when I read the newspapers, when I see the suicide killings on television day after day. That hurts. Some in the media call them "kamikaze," which is wrong. The kamikaze attacked only military targets, never civilians. But these suicide killers murder children and their mothers and their grandmothers. You read the stories of *how* they kill and it breaks your heart. And then I say to myself, maybe I was wrong in supporting the Oslo Agreement, maybe I was naive. They don't want us there. And then . . . I close my eyes.

**And then . . . ?**

Then I say we cannot accept that as the final answer. I am not giving up on humanity, not even on the killers' humanity. I don't even give up on those parents who today are encouraging their children to commit suicide by killing other children. I think it's possible to talk. But the first thing must be the removal of this blasphemy. It is a blasphemy to kill children and their parents in the name of the Koran.

**You said you have suggested a convening of religious persons. Why do you feel that this could be an answer?**

Because the terrorists invoke religious arguments. Only religious authorities could effectively tell them these arguments are wrong and should be repudiated. But if these religious authorities encourage their followers to kill by committing suicide, it will never work.

**Would they do this on the assumption that over a long enough period of time it will drive the Israelis away?**

I think Hamas and the other terrorist organizations are convinced that Israel will be tired at the end and give up. They are wrong. We have not waited 2,000 years in exile and made so many sacrifices to have a very small nation in an ocean of Islam in order to give it up. The great philosopher Nachmanides said that if you want proof that God exists, look at the Jewish people. They're still here. That means God is protecting us.

You know, I was in Verona last weekend, and there was an arena and somebody said to me, "This arena is 2,000 years old and it is almost intact." And I said, "Look, I work for a people who have no arenas, only a book. And that book is intact."

# Afterword

THERE IS A marvelous anecdote in Hasidic literature that recounts how a young student came to Rebbe Mendel of Kotzk and said, "Master, I am terribly disappointed in God." "Why?" "I'll tell you why," said this student. "It took him six days to create the world, and look at it. It's terrible." So the master said, "Tell me, could you do better?" And the student, not knowing why, said, "Yes." And the master said, "In that case, then, what are you waiting for? Start doing it."

BOOKS BY ELIE WIESEL


ALL RIVERS RUN TO THE SEA

This first volume of Wiesel's memoirs recalls in intimate detail the experiences that shaped his life—from the small Carpathian village where he was born to the horrors of Auschwitz and Buchenwald to his discovery of his calling as a writer and "Messenger to Mankind."

0-8052-1028-8 SCHOCKEN


AND THE SEA IS NEVER FULL

The concluding volume of Wiesel's memoirs opens in 1969 as the author sets himself a challenge: "I will become militant. I will teach, share, bear witness. I will reveal and try to mitigate the victim's solitude." He makes words his weapons, and in these pages we watch as he meets with world leaders, returns to Auschwitz, and travels to regions ruled by war, dictatorship, and racism in order to engage the most pressing issues of our day.

0-8052-1029-6 SCHOCKEN

## A BEGGAR IN JERUSALEM

In the days following the Six-Day War, a Holocaust survivor visits the reunited city of Jerusalem. At the Western Wall he encounters the beggars and madmen who congregate there every evening, and who force him to confront the ghosts of his past and his ties to the present.

0-8052-1052-0   SCHOCKEN

## CONVERSATIONS WITH ELIE WIESEL

Elie Wiesel's voice has long been a beacon of humanity and wisdom in our volatile and violent times. In these conversations with the host of the public television series *The Open Mind*, he speaks about the subjects closest to his heart: memory, compassion, nationalism, the anatomy of hate, capital punishment, the role of the state, and tolerance.

0-8052-1141-1   SCHOCKEN

## THE FIFTH SON

When the son of a Holocaust prisoner discovers his brooding father has been haunted by his role in a murder of a brutal S.S. officer just after the war, the son also discovers that the Nazi is still alive. What begins as a quest for his father's love becomes a reenactment of the past, as the son sets out to complete his father's act of revenge.

0-8052-1083-0   SCHOCKEN

## THE FORGOTTEN

A distinguished psychotherapist and Holocaust survivor is losing his memory to an incurable disease. Never having spoken of the war years before, he resolves to tell his son about his past—the heroic parts as well as the parts that fill him with shame—before it is too late.

0-8052-1019-9   SCHOCKEN

## FROM THE KINGDOM OF MEMORY

The essays and speeches collected here include reminiscences of Wiesel's life before the Holocaust and his struggle to find meaning afterward, his impassioned testimony at the Klaus Barbie trial, his plea to President Reagan not to visit a German S.S. cemetery, and his speech in acceptance of the Nobel Peace Prize.

0-8052-1020-2   SCHOCKEN

## THE GATES OF THE FOREST

A young Jew hiding from the Nazis in the forests and small towns of Eastern Europe allows another refugee to sacrifice himself in his stead. As he struggles with his guilt, one question recurs: How to live in a world that God has abandoned?

0-8052-1044-X   SCHOCKEN

## A JEW TODAY

In this powerful collection of essays, letters, and diary entries, Wiesel probes such central moral and political issues as Zionism and the Middle East conflict, anti-Semitism in the former U.S.S.R., the obligations of American Jews toward Israel, and the media's treatment of the Holocaust.

0-394-74057-2   VINTAGE

## THE JUDGES

A plane is forced down by bad weather, and its five passengers find refuge in a nearby house. But then their host begins to interrogate them—forcing them to face the truth and meaning of their lives—and announces that the least worthy among them will die. A compelling novel that reflects the philosophical, religious, and moral questions that are at the heart of Wiesel's work.

0-375-40909-2   KNOPF

### THE OATH

A Christian boy disappears from a village in the Carpathian Mountains and the Jews are accused of ritual murder. They gather and swear that whoever survives the pogrom that is certain to follow will never speak of what has happened. But fifty years later, when the sole survivor meets a man whose life might be saved by hearing what had been promised to silence, the survivor is forced to make a heartwrenching decision.

0-8052-0808-9   SCHOCKEN

### THE TESTAMENT

On August 12, 1952, Russia's greatest Jewish writers were secretly executed by Stalin. In this novel, poet Paltiel Kossover meets the same fate but, unlike his historical counterparts, he is permitted to leave behind a written testament. Two decades later, Paltiel's son reads this precious record and finds that it illuminates the shadowed planes of his own life.

0-8052-1115-2   SCHOCKEN

### THE TOWN BEYOND THE WALL

Based on Wiesel's own life, this is the story of a young Holocaust survivor who returns to his hometown after the liberation, seeking to understand the mystery of what he calls "the face in the window"—the symbol of all those who just stood by and watched as innocent men, women, and children were led to the slaughter.

0-8052-1045-8   SCHOCKEN

## THE TRIAL OF GOD

When three itinerant actors arrive in a small Eastern European village to perform a Purim play for the Jewish community, they are horrified to discover that all but two of the Jewish residents have been murdered in a recent pogrom. The actors decide to stage a mock trial of God, indicting Him for allowing such things to happen to His children.

0-8052-1053-9   SCHOCKEN

## TWILIGHT

The story of a man whose search for a friend who saved him during the Holocaust leads him to question the very meaning of survival, this novel of memory, loss, and madness resonates with the dramatic upheavals of our century.

0-8052-1058-X   SCHOCKEN